Dear
Victoria,
Perhaps another
skill to learn?
Love Charlotte

MARCH 2008

MAKING TEDDY BEARS

MAKING TEDDY BEARS

JOYCE LUCKIN

B.T. BATSFORD LTD • LONDON

To my family: John, Carolynne, Christopher and Valerie with love

First published 1995

© Joyce Luckin, 1995
Original illustrations by Barbara Richardson
Patterns © Joyce Luckin, 1995

Printed in Hong Kong

Published by
B.T. Batsford Ltd
4 Fitzhardinge Street
London W1H 0AH

A catalogue record for this book is available from the British Library

ISBN 0 7134 7359 2

Contents

Introduction

Bears have existed as children's toys for centuries, but the prototype for the teddy bear we all know and love today was created in 1902 by Margarete Steiff (1847-1909).

This remarkable craftswoman, who lived in a small village called Giengen-an-der-Brenz in Germany, was confined to a wheelchair after contracting polio at the age of two. Initially she earned her living by dressmaking. With little pieces of leftover material she also used to make animal-shaped pincushions which she later decided to adapt into toys to give to children.

THE ORIGINS OF THE TEDDY BEAR

Over the years she was able to give up dressmaking, which she did not enjoy, and concentrate on making soft toys, eventually taking on some employees to help her to meet the growing orders. Some time in 1902, inspired by her nephew's sketches of the brown bears in Stuttgart Zoo, she designed and made some lovely stuffed plush bears with rounded ears, long curved arms, large feet and a slight hump on their backs. When the bears were sent to the Leipzig Trade Fair in 1903 they met with great excitement. An American from the George Borgfeldt Company ordered 3,000 bears on the spot. As a result Margarete Steiff had to enlarge her premises and take on more workers. Before the order was complete it was doubled. In 1907, five years after the first bear was made, Steiff manufactured over 950,000 bears, employing 400 factory workers and 1800 outworkers. Although Margarete Steiff died two years later, the original Steiff bears are still much sought after today and highly valued by collectors around the world.

It is commonly believed that the teddy bear owes

its name to President Theodore or 'Teddy' Roosevelt. In late 1902, a cartoon by Clifford Berryman appeared in the Washington Post. It showed the President, who had apparently taken time out to hunt while on a visit to the southern States to settle a territorial dispute, refusing to kill a tethered bear cub. A Russian immigrant shopkeeper by the name of Morris Michtom saw the cartoon and wrote to the President to ask whether he would object to the name 'Teddy's Bear' being given to the little bears his wife made to supplement their income. Although the President could not imagine this increasing their sales, he nevertheless gave his permission and the first 'Teddy's Bear', which sat in the window of Michtom's shop beside a copy of the cartoon, proved to be an instant success. With this incentive Morris Michtom founded the Ideal Toy and Novelty Company of America, manufacturing teddy bears and other soft toys in great quantities. No letters to substantiate this appealing story have ever been found, but the name has remained ever since and on the strength of the teddy bear, Michtom's company continued to trade until 1982.

Before 1914 most soft toy manufacturers were German although a few bear makers, such as 'Terry'er Toys' and Farnell, were operating in Britain as early as the 1890s. Sadly, neither of these companies is now in business but during the 1920s and 1930s countless others sprang up to take their place throughout Britain, Europe and the United States as the craze for bears gathered steam. One of the companies established around 1930 and still in operation today is Merrythought (an old English word meaning wishbone), which is among Britain's largest soft toy manufacturers.

Early bears were made of mohair plush, which is a fabric obtained from the long, silky hair of the Angora goat, and were stuffed with wood-wool (wood shavings previously used for packing delicate objects). They had wooden boot-button eyes, and later, glass-beaded eyes. In 1908 the first 'growlers' were inserted. Felt was used for paw pads, while joints were constructed of cardboard discs held together with a metal pin and strengthened with a metal washer.

TEDDY BEAR MAKING TODAY

All the necessary materials for making teddy bears are now readily available at craft shops and tend to be both safer and more durable than in the past. Easy-to-use plastic safety eyes, plastic joints which simply clip together and polyester stuffing can be bought to give even the simplest of home-made bears a professionally-crafted look and moveable arms and legs. There is also a wide range of mohair and fine fur fabric on the market so whatever the colour or texture you can be sure of finding the right material for the bear you have in mind.

Today there are festivals, exhibitions, sales, concerts, conventions and gatherings for bear collectors or 'arctophiles' (meaning a friend of the bear), and makers all over the world. In the United States bears are extremely popular and interest continues to grow in Britain. Smaller companies and professionals who design and make bears by hand are ofen referred to as 'bear artists'.

THE BEARS IN THIS BOOK

I have put together a selection of teddy bear patterns in this book. They are mostly my own designs, although a few, whose origins are now forgotten, have been modified several times by me over the years. All my bears have been given names and each one has been carefully photographed so you can see exactly how it should look. I always maintain, whenever I give talks, that if you can thread a needle and push it through a piece of cloth, you can make a bear. Even my grandchildren, one of whom is only six years old, have been able to make bears from some of the patterns featured in this book.

The secret of good bear making is in the stuffing, which must always be firm and evenly packed. Take a wooden spoon and, with the bowl fitting snugly in the palm of your hand, use the handle for pushing small pieces of polyester stuffing into position. If you do it properly, you can expect the stuffing of the bear to take longer than any other part of the making process. Another useful hint is to experiment with the position of the eyes using black glass-headed pins, moving them around until you have found the right expression. The general guidelines in the next chapter are relevant to all the bears and you should read them carefully before making a start. Finally, all the materials and component parts for the bears in this book were obtained from Oakley Fabrics, 8 May Street, Luton, Bedfordshire LU1 3QY, who will send samples on request and always execute mail orders very promptly. However, you should find that most local craft shops and large department stores stock all the necessary materials.

Before you begin

To keep instructions to a minimum, the following information applies to all the bears. Read it through carefully before you start and, if you are unsure of any of the techniques, try one of the easier bears first of all.

PATTERN PIECES

Arrows on the pattern pieces indicate the direction of the pile. If you are not sure of this, stroke the fabric and when it lies flat and smooth that is the downward direction.

The pattern pieces should be stitched together as close to the outer edges as possible to prevent the fabric from fraying. Narrow seam widths have been allowed for on each pattern piece.

With some of the bears I have marked a cross on the pattern piece to indicate the best position for the eyes. With the others, try placing glass-headed pins in different positions before securing the safety eyes, as they can completely alter the expression of a face. The lower down you place the eyes, the younger the bear will look.

In some cases I have marked the correct position for the ears with a dotted line on the pattern piece. Elsewhere, place the ears where you feel they would look best. To attach them to the head, you should cut two slits of the right size after consulting the pattern. Put the oversewn raw edge of the ear through and stitch through the head and ear material.

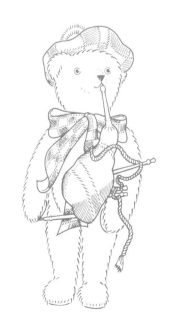

SEWING

Sew with strong thread, doubled if hand stitching. I always stitch by hand as the fabric has a tendency to 'walk' when sewn by machine so has to be pinned and tacked beforehand.

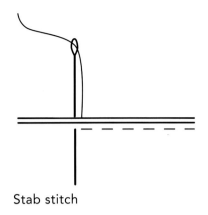

Stab stitch

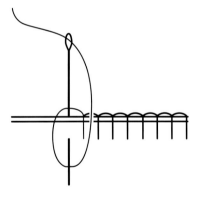

Overstitch

Blanket stitch

As long as you are careful and don't try to rush, either method will produce good results. Use stab stitch except when drawing openings together when you can oversew with the right sides facing or use button hole or blanket stitch (see left). Always fasten off seams with at least four stitches to secure them.

FABRIC

When cutting fur fabric or mohair snip from the back with the tips of sharp scissors so that the pile is not cut away in great chunks. Never press fur fabric or felt.

When sewing always stroke the pile back to the right side of the fabric with a needle so that it hides the seams.

Use the best fabrics you can afford but do not be afraid to use materials other than those mentioned. Old tweed skirts or camel-coloured coats and even discarded corduroy trousers and velvet curtains make excellent bears as long as they are for your own family.

Fur fabric and mohair are sold at the standard width of 137 cm (54 in). Therefore, only the necessary length of fabric is given in each relevant materials list to avoid repetition.

SEAMS

After finishing a seam, always go over it gently with a few strokes from a teasle brush to hide it completely. This is especially important with oversewn seams.

STUFFING

Stuff the head and limbs in the correct order and always stuff the body last. Pack the stuffing in very firmly, particularly around the neck and shoulders to prevent the head from wobbling, shaping carefully as you work. Care taken at this point will ensure that the bear has an attractive and well proportioned appearance rather than simply being a jumble of parts sewn together.

As a rough indication of the amounts of polyester stuffing needed for each bear, you can expect to use the following:

HEIGHT OF BEAR		AMOUNT OF STUFFING	
cm	ins	g	oz
50	20	795	28
43	17	680	24
38	15	455	16
30	12	340	12
28	11	285	10
23	9	115	4
18	7	85	3

SAFETY REGULATIONS

If you are making bears to sell, always get some form of documentation from your supplier to state that the materials you have chosen meet the requirements of Safety Standard BS 5665 (see pages 70-71). This should not be a problem as reputable suppliers will expect you to ask for it.

Always sew in a label showing a CE mark and your name and postcode so that you can be traced if necessary. You can also put your address if you wish. It is sensible to mark the bear as being unsuitable for children under three years of age just to safeguard yourself. Bear artists usually state that their bears are for collectors only. Make sure you do conform to safety regulations before sewing in the label.

For further information on the EC regulations governing safety and the correct use of fabrics, polyester stuffing and other component parts, refer to pages 70-71.

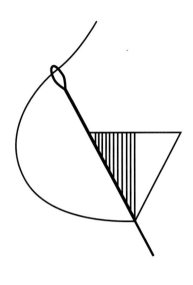

Stitching the nose and mouth

EYES AND JOINTS

When fixing safety eyes, make sure that they are firmly embedded in the fabric so that tiny teeth and fingers cannot prise them out. To do this, first find and mark the position in which you wish to attach them. Then push a small hole in the material with the point of a pair of sharp scissors. Push the eyes through the material and fix securely in place on the other side with a washer. Take equal care to ensure that joints are also safely attached (always check the back of the packet as instructions may vary slightly between brands). Plastic eyes and joints are obtainable from good craft shops and large department stores.

To embroider the nose, push a large needle threaded with black wool or embroidery cotton through from the back of the material. Work outwards from the central point counting the number of stitches you make and repeat on the other side. This gives the nose a symmetrical appearance.

MAKING A POMPON

Both Rob Roy and Ramsay have pompons attached to their tam-o'-shanters. The pompons can be made as follows.

Cut two circles of card 4 cm (1 5/8 in) in diameter. Put the point of a pair of scissors in the centre of each card to make an inner circle 2.5 cm (1 in) in diameter.

Place the two pieces of card together and wind the wool round them until the inner hole is completely filled. With the tips of the scissors cut through the wool on the outer edge and, separating the cards slightly, tie a length of wool tightly between the two to hold all the strands together.

Tear the pieces of card away and trim the edges of the pompon evenly. Sew the pompon on to the right side of the tam-o'-shanter.

TIPS

If you are making more than one bear from a pattern, it is a good idea to cut the pieces from card (I use old cereal packets). Punch a hole in each piece and tie them together leaving enough cord to allow you to draw round the pattern on the back of the material. This will prevent any of the pattern pieces from getting lost. Transfer all the information from the patterns in the book to your own copies and look out for pieces that should also be cut in reverse.

It is better to start a bear when you feel in the mood, rather than waiting until you have bought the correct materials or you risk losing the impetus. However, do make sure that all the fabrics and component parts you use are suitable for the job.

The level of difficulty varies with each bear. If you have never made one before you could start with Christabel and Valentine as they are the simplest to make. Then move on to Holly and follow with Oliver who has no joints to fix or William who has only arm joints. Save Joseph and Georgie until you have had a little practice. David is probably the most complicated of all because of the construction of his head. Once you get the hang of it you will be able to make any of the bears quickly and easily. It can be fun to mix and match different pattern pieces to create a totally unique bear. I have provided some ideas at the end of the book and have tried them all myself with good results.

Once you have successfully made a bear you will want to go on and on. Good luck and enjoy your bear making!

CHRISTABEL

The following four bears make ideal Christmas gifts, or you could use them as decorations, along with some red bows, for a tree that will delight the entire family.

Christabel is the simplest bear to make in the book, consisting of only three pattern pieces. She measures 17cm (6 ¾ in) high and I have chosen to make her from short-pile fur fabric, although corduroy, velvet, felt or coloured cotton are all equally suitable. This bear has a small bell sewn to each hand, which gave me the inspiration for her name.

MATERIALS

36 cm (14 1/8 in) x 17.5 cm (7 in) fabric of your choice

1 pair of safety eyes 5 mm (1/4 in) in diameter

length of black wool or embroidery cotton for nose and mouth

handful of polyester stuffing

46 cm (18 1/8 in) of 1 cm (3/8 in) wide ribbon

2 small bells

INSTRUCTIONS

1. Cut out the body pieces from fabric

2. Pin the two front pieces, right sides together, from the central point of the head to the top of the inner legs and stitch a seam. Pin the front section of the body to the back and stitch right around the bear starting at A and finishing at B. This should leave an opening down one side for turning and stuffing

3. Turn the bear right side out and attach the safety eyes as marked on the pattern piece

4. Embroider the nose and mouth

5. Stuff the bear firmly (except for the ears). Stitch across the tops of the legs and arms to allow the bear to be placed in a sitting position and across the bottom of the ears to define them

6. Overstitch the opening at the side

7. If using fur fabric, trim the snout, inner ears and paws

8. Tie a ribbon round the bear's neck and sew a bell to each paw

HOLLY

Holly is also very easy to make. You should use colourful cotton with a small print for her playsuit. This is the perfect bear to make for very young children - even her eyes are embroidered, so there is no chance of tiny fingers or teeth prying anything loose.

MATERIALS

23 cm (9 in) x 26 cm (10 1/4 in) printed cotton

23 cm (9 in) x 23 cm (9 in) felt

length of black wool or embroidery cotton for eyes, nose and mouth

handful of polyester stuffing

25 cm (9 3/4 in) of 1 cm (3/8 in) wide ribbon

INSTRUCTIONS

1. Cut a piece of cotton measuring 9 cm (3 1/2 in) x 22 cm (8 3/4 in) for the body. Fold it in half with right sides together to form a rectangle 9 cm (3 1/2 in) x 11cm (4 3/8 in)

2. Stitch the 9 cm (3 1/2 in) side opposite the fold leaving a small opening for turning right side out and stuffing. You can then turn the side seam around until it forms centre back

3. Gather the top with running stitches and fasten off at a width of 4 cm (1 5/8 in). Gather the bottom of the body and fasten off at a width of 7.5cm (3 in). Turn the body right side out and tuck the bottom corners up inside to accommodate the feet as marked on the pattern piece. Leave 2.5 cm (1 in) between the feet

4. Cut a second piece of cotton 5 cm (2 in) x 12.5 cm (5 in) and fold it in half lengthways for the arms. Stitch along one long edge on the wrong side, turn right side out and then stuff

5. Cut out the pattern pieces for the head and ears in felt. With right sides together, pin and stitch the gusset to the sides of the head matching the pointed end to the nose. Stitch from nose to neck

6. With right sides together, stitch round the outer edge of the ears. Turn them right side out and oversew the inner edges. Make two cuts on the head, as indicated on the pattern piece, to accommodate the ears and stitch them in position

7. Turn the head right side out and embroider the eyes, nose and mouth. Stuff the head firmly

8. Cut out the paws and feet from felt and stitch round the curved edges with right sides together. Carefully turn them right side out and stuff

9. Turn the ends of the arms under and attach the paws with small, neat stitches. Stitch the feet in position at the bottom corners of the body

10. Stuff the body and oversew the opening

11. Oversew the head to the arm strip, turning the rough edge under as you stitch to make a neat seam. Then stitch the arm strip to the body, making sure both it and the head are secure

12. Sew a ribbon bow to Holly between her arms and body

NOEL

Proudly wearing a green rosette to show that he came second in a competition, Noel is the star of this quartet. He stands 15 cm (6 in) high and is slightly more difficult to make than the first two bears in the book.

MATERIALS

40 cm(15 3/4 in) x 28 cm (11 in) short-pile fur fabric

small piece of felt for pads

length of black wool or embroidery cotton for nose and mouth

handful of polyester stuffing

1 pair of safety eyes 4 mm (1/8 in) in diameter

4 safety eyes 1.5 cm (5/8 in) in diameter (to use as joints)

45 cm (17 3/4 in) of 1 cm (3/8 in) or 2 cm (3/4 in) wide ribbon for his neck

60 cm (23 5/8 in) of 5 mm (1/4 in) green ribbon to make the rosette

1 small gold safety pin

INSTRUCTIONS

1. Cut out all the pattern pieces in fabric, remembering to cut the relevant pieces in reverse

2. With right sides together, stitch the head gusset to the sides of the head matching the square end to the nose. Stitch from nose to neck

3. Stitch round the curved edge of the ears on the wrong side, turn them right side out and oversew the straight edge

4. Place the ears at each side of the bear's head, pin them in your preferred position and then stitch in place. Turn the head right side out

5. Using glass-headed pins, establish the best position for the safety eyes and then fasten them securely

6. Embroider the nose and mouth

7. Stuff the head firmly

8. With right sides together, pin the two body pieces and stitch leaving the neck edge open. Turn right side out

9. Pin the leg pieces with right sides together and stitch leaving an opening at the back for turning and stuffing. Repeat with the second leg

10. Cut out and position the felt sole. Stitch it in place on the wrong side of the fabric and then turn the leg right side out. Repeat with the second sole

11. To construct each arm, first pin the felt paw to the forearm with right sides together. Stitch in place

12. Pin the forearm (now with the paw attached) to the back of the arm and stitch the two pieces together leaving an opening for turning

13. Turn the arms right side out and fasten both the arms and legs into the body using the safety eyes as joints. Place the arms 1.5 cm (5/8 in) from the neck and the legs 2 cm (3/4 in) from the bottom of the body. Push the shanks through into the body and secure them with washers

14. Stuff the arms, legs and body (in that order) and overstitch all the open seams. Oversew the head to the body, turning the rough edges under as you stitch to make a neat seam. Use doubled thread for this purpose and stitch round the neck twice to ensure that the head is really secure

15. Tie a ribbon round Noel's neck

HOW TO MAKE THE ROSETTE

1. Halve the green ribbon and cut 4 cm (1 5/8 in) from each piece

2. Join the ends of one half to form a circle and gather along one long edge with running stitch. Draw up the ribbon to form a small roundel and secure with several stitches. Repeat with the second half but do not draw it up quite so tightly

3. Stitch the smaller roundel on top of the larger one. Place both 4 cm (1 5/8 in) pieces of ribbon side by side at the back and stitch in position

4. Sew a safety pin to the back

JOSEPH

This bear is a little fiddly, so you may prefer not to attempt him until you have had some more practice. He is best made in felt, velvet or, if you attempt short-pile mohair as I did, be prepared to work very hard at preventing him from fraying as you sew. Joseph is a challenge.

MATERIALS

32 cm (12 5/8 in) x 40 cm (15 3/4 in) suitable fabric

small piece of brown felt for soles of feet

length of black wool or embroidery cotton for mouth and nose

small handful of polyester stuffing

1 pair of safety eyes 3 mm (1/8 in) in diameter or 2 small black beads

4 safety eyes 1 cm (3/8 in) in diameter for joints

30 cm (11 3/4 in) of 5 mm (1/4 in) wide ribbon

INSTRUCTIONS

1. Cut out all the pattern pieces from the fabric, remembering to cut pieces in reverse where necessary

2. Stitch the head gusset to the sides of the head, fitting the narrower curved end to the nose. Sew from nose to neck

3. Stitch round the curved edge of each ear leaving the inner edge open. Turn the ears right side out and oversew the straight edge

4. Pin the ears to the sides of the head in your preferred position and stitch in place. Turn the head right side out

5. Embroider the nose and mouth and, using black, glass-headed pins, find the right position for the eyes. Secure the safety eyes or, if you prefer, you can embroider the eyes or sew on small black beads

6. Stuff the head firmly

7. Stitch the arm pieces together on the wrong side of the fabric leaving an opening for turning and stuffing. Turn the arms right side out

8. Pin the leg pieces with right sides together and stitch the seams leaving a space at the back of each leg for turning and stuffing

9. Position the felt soles and stitch them in place on the wrong side of the fabric. Turn the legs right side out.

You might find this a tricky process but it can be done with patience. Using the blunt end of a knitting needle helps

10. Stitch the body gusset to the front edge of each body side and then stitch the back body seam leaving an opening for fixing the joints and stuffing. Turn the body right side out

11. Attach the arms and legs to the body using the safety eyes as joints. Position the arms 1 cm (3/8 in) from the neck edge and the legs 1 cm (3/8 in) from the bottom of the body pushing the shanks through into the body

12. Stuff the legs, arms and body (in that order) and oversew all the openings

13. Carefully oversew the stuffed head to the body using doubled thread, turning the rough edges under as you stitch to make a neat seam

14. Tie a ribbon round Joseph's neck and he is complete

VALENTINE

This bear was designed to hold a small gift for Valentine's Day and appeared on television with Una Stubbs and myself on the programme This Morning. He looks fine in fur fabric, corduroy, velvet or even felt, and is simple to make.

MATERIALS

42 cm (16 1/2 in) x 25 cm (9 3/4 in) suitable fabric

small piece of felt for soles of feet

length of black wool or embroidery cotton for nose and mouth

handful of polyester stuffing

1 pair of safety eyes 1 cm (3/8 in) in diameter

50 cm (19 3/4 in) of 2.5 cm (1 in) wide ribbon

18 cm (7 in) x 8 cm (3 1/8 in) cotton or rayon material for lining

INSTRUCTIONS

1. Cut out all the pattern pieces, remembering to cut one of the front sections in reverse

2. With right sides together, pin and stitch the gusset to the sides of the head matching the pointed end to the nose. Then sew the body seam at centre front - from the nose to the top of the legs

3. With right sides together, pin and stitch the top and bottom back body sections to the front of the bear

4. Pin and stitch the felt soles into position

5. Turn the bear right side out

6. Fasten the safety eyes in position and embroider the nose and mouth

7. Stuff the head firmly, leaving out the ears but just stitching across them to mark their position. Next stuff the legs, arms and body (in that order)

8. Take the lining material and pin one edge to the bottom of the upper section of the body with right sides together. Stitch carefully together. Now pin and sew the lining material to the edge of the lower section of the body. This is a little tricky, but once you have pushed the lining material gently inside the bear's body so that the right side of the fabric shows, you will have created a little pocket in which to place a small gift

9. Tie a ribbon around Valentine's neck

OLIVER

During the Second World War there was neither the time nor the money to manufacture soft toys for children. Creative parents and grandparents came to the rescue, sorting through their cast off clothes and rag-bags to find suitable materials. Oliver is based on a pattern from 1940, which I changed slightly to give a more shapely foot. He is simple to make and looks good in almost any fabric. If you wish, even his eyes can be of embroidered felt. He is 30.5 cm (12 in) high.

MATERIALS

53 cm (21 in) x 28 cm (11 in) of suitable fabric

felt for soles of feet and paws

length of black wool or embroidery cotton for nose and mouth

small quantity of polyester stuffing or, if you want to achieve a really authentic 1940 effect, snip up old nylons into small pieces for stuffing

1 pair of safety eyes 5 mm (1/4 in) in diameter or, alternatively, you can use small pieces of embroidered felt for the eyes

45 cm (17 3/4 in) of 2.5 cm (1 in) wide ribbon

INSTRUCTIONS

1. Cut out all the pattern pieces in fabric. Remember, when cutting out the pattern for the body and legs, to double the material and place the fold line on the paper pattern piece against the fold in the material

2. Stitch the gusset to the sides of the head, matching the rounded end to the nose. Stitch from nose to neck

3. With right sides together, stitch the curved edge of each ear, turn them right side out and oversew the slightly curved inner edge

4. Stitch the ears on to the head leaving 6.5 cm (2 1/2 in) between them. Turn the head right side out

5. The eyes should be placed roughly 3.5 cm (1 1/2 in) from the nose. As an alternative to using 5 mm (1/4 in) safety eyes, you could embroider a few white stitches in the centres of two small circles of black felt, attach them to slightly larger circles of brown felt and stitch them to the face

6. Embroider the nose and mouth or sew on a small circle of black felt for the nose

7. Stuff the head firmly

8. To separate the legs, cut along the fold from the bottom of the pattern piece to the dotted line

Open out the body and legs and then refold and pin them (right sides together) so that the body fold line is at centre front and the two slots are at either side for the arms. Stitch from the top to the dotted line, forming a seam at centre back. Pin and sew each leg seam separately

9. Pin and stitch the upper part of each foot to the bottom of the leg on the wrong side of the fabric. Pin and stitch the felt soles to the feet

10. Fold each arm in half with right sides together and stitch leaving the straight end open. Stitch the arms to the body

11. Turn the body, legs and arms right side out. Gather the neck edge of the body slightly so that the opening matches that of the head

12. Stuff the legs and stitch along the dotted line to allow them to bend

13. Stuff the arms firmly and then the body. Oversew the head to the body with doubled thread, turning the rough edges in as you stitch to make a neat seam

14. Finally, tie a ribbon round Oliver's neck

PAUL

I named this bear after a young friend called Paul who kept him as a constant companion throughout his childhood. Safe and cuddly for a young child, Paul is easy to make and stands at 40.5 cm (16 in) high.

MATERIALS

76 cm (30 in) x 30.5 cm (12 in) of sturdy fabric for the body

25 cm (10 in) washable short-pile fur fabric for the head, paws and feet

length of black wool or embroidery cotton for nose and mouth

230 g (8 oz) of polyester stuffing

1 pair of safety eyes 1 cm (3/8 in) in diameter

98 cm (38 1/2 in) of 2.5 cm (1 in) wide ribbon for the neck

INSTRUCTIONS

1. Cut out the head from fur fabric, using the pattern from Timothy (see page 93) but adding 2.5 cm (1 in) at the neck end

2. Cut out the feet and paw pieces also from fur fabric

3. Form the head as instructed in Timothy's pattern (see page 46)

4. With right sides together, pin and stitch round the curved edges of the feet and paws. Turn them right side out, stuff and overstitch the straight edges

5. Fold the fabric for the body in half with right sides together and sew part way along the open short side (by hand or machine using stab/running stitch (see page 12)). Leave 10 cm (4 in) open at the top of the seam and make a cut of exactly the same length down the fold line on the opposite short side. Leave both the top and bottom (the longer sides) of the rectangle open. This should make an open-ended bag measuring roughly 37 cm (14 5/8 in) x 30 cm (13 in)

6. Pin and stitch the paws at either side, 4 cm (1 1/2 in) down from each top corner. (The paws should be pointing inside the bag, so that when the body is turned they will be facing outwards.) Now stitch the remaining 4 cm (1 1/2 in) above each paw

7. Pin and stitch the feet at the bottom corners of the bag. As with the paws, the feet must be pointing inside at this stage. Gather the material in-between the feet and secure at a width of roughly 6 cm (2 3/8 in)

8. Gather the top edge of the body to fit snugly around the head and then turn it right side out. Stuff the body lightly to make it soft and cuddly

9. Having stuffed the head, stitch it firmly to the body with doubled thread. This is a little tricky, so first pin the head to the opening, turning the rough edges under to give a neat seam

10. Tie a ribbon round Paul's neck

KIRSTY

I made Kirsty for a young girl who had fallen in love with Paul's bear. She is really a duplicate of Paul except that you should use thinner, patterned cotton material for her body. To make sure she is just as hard-wearing as Paul, the material should be lined with a piece of calico or sheeting of the same dimensions. Simply pin the lining to the outer material and sew them as one. You will also need 46 cm (18 in) of narrow ribbon to make bows in her ears and 1 m (40 in) of 5 cm (2 in) wide lace to be gathered and sewn around the bottom edge of her body. In every other respect Kirsty is made in the same way as Paul and the two complement each other perfectly.

BRUMAS

I designed and named Brumas after the polar bear born many years ago in London Zoo. Just as the real Brumas became a very popular attraction at the Zoo, this bear, made in white fur fabric, is bound to delight everyone he meets. He is simple and quick to make and would be a good bear to start with as he has no joints or gussets. He stands on all fours at a height of 25.5 cm (10 in).

MATERIALS

46 cm (18 1/8 in) of white or cream fur fabric

small piece of fawn or pink felt for soles of feet

length of black wool or embroidery cotton for the nose

455 g (1 lb) of polyester stuffing

1 pair of safety eyes 1 cm (3/8 in) in diameter

INSTRUCTIONS

1. Before cutting out the pattern pieces in fur fabric, join the paper patterns for the front and back sections of the body along the line A-B to make a whole piece. Cut two of these body pieces in fur fabric, remembering to cut one of them in reverse

2. When cutting out the underbody, you need to double the fabric and place the fold line of the underbody pattern up against the fold in the fabric. Cut out the head and ears in fur fabric and the soles of the feet in felt

3. With right sides together, pin and stitch the head pieces leaving the neck edge open

4. With right sides together, pin and stitch round the curved edge of each ear. Turn the ears right side out and overstitch the straight edge

5. Stitch the ears in place and turn the head right side out. Fasten in the safety eyes and embroider the nose

6. Stitch the darts as marked on the underbody pattern. Then pin and stitch the underbody to the front and back sections of the upper body. Leave the seam along the bear's back open for turning and stuffing

7. Stitch the soles into the feet and turn the body right side out

8. Next, carefully pin and sew the head on to the body with doubled thread, turning the rough edges under as you stitch

9. Stuff the legs, body and head firmly and overstitch the back seam, turning the edges of the fabric in a fraction as you work to make a neat join

10. Brumas is now complete and ready to be admired just like his namesake before him

GEORGIE

Georgie is a rather special bear because he won a first in a competition and proudly sports his blue rosette. At the time he was also wearing a brown ribbon with white spots, which he has kept ever since. He stands 18 cm (7 in) high and is perfect in every detail. Unlike Noel (see page 20), who is a second prize winner, Georgie's head turns, which is just as well because it was a little turned when he won his first award.

MATERIALS

42 cm (16 1/2 in) x 30 cm (11 3/4 in) short-pile fur fabric

small piece of suede or felt for the paws and soles of the feet

length of black wool or embroidery cotton for nose and mouth

two handfuls of polyester stuffing

1 pair of safety eyes 1 cm (3/8 in) in diameter

5 safety eyes 1.5 cm (5/8 in) in diameter (to use as joints)

45 cm (17 3/4 in) of narrow spotted ribbon for the neck

60 cm (23 5/8 in) narrow blue ribbon for the rosette

small gold safety pin

INSTRUCTIONS

1. Cut out the pattern pieces in fabric, not forgetting those to be cut in reverse

2. Cut out the paws and soles in suede or felt

3. With right sides together, pin and stitch the gusset to the sides of the head matching the pointed end to the nose. Leave 2.5 cm (1 in) open on one seam at the back of the head to allow you to insert the joint and stuff the head. Sew from nose to neck

4. With right sides together, stitch round the curved outer edge of each ear, turn right side out and then oversew the inner edge

5. Attach the ears to the head in the position indicated by the dotted line on the pattern piece

6. Turn the head right side out

7. Secure the safety eyes in a suitable position and then embroider the nose and mouth. Trim the pile away to form the snout

8. Stuff the head lightly

9. Stitch the straight edge of the paw to the forearm and repeat for the second forearm

10. Placing right sides together, stitch the forearms to the back of the arms leaving a small opening on the back seam for turning

11. With right sides together, pin and stitch the leg pieces leaving an opening on the back seam for turning

12. Sew the soles into position and turn the legs and arms right side out

13. Pin and stitch the front of the body to the two side pieces with right sides together. Sew the back seam leaving an opening of 5 cm (2 in) for fixing washers to joints and stuffing. Turn the body right side out

14. Gather the neck ends of the head and body. Attach the head to the body using an eye as a joint. Push the shank through into the neck of the body and secure with a washer. Finish stuffing the head firmly and oversew the opening at the back of the head

15. Attach the arms 2.5 cm (1 in) below the neck and the legs 2.5 cm (1 in) from the bottom of the body using the safety eyes as joints. Push the shanks through into the body and secure with washers

16. Stuff the legs, arms and body firmly (in that order) and oversew the openings

17. Pin the rosette on to the bear and tie a ribbon round his neck

ROSETTE

Make the rosette following the instructions given on page 20

BERTIE

Bertie is designed in the style of a 1962 bear. At 25 cm (10 in) high, he makes an ideal companion for a larger bear and is just the right size for a small child's hand. He is named after a favourite beagle of mine.

MATERIALS

30 cm (11 3/4 in) x 40 cm (15 3/4 in) of short-pile fur fabric

small piece of suede or felt for the paws and soles

length of black wool or embroidery cotton for the nose and mouth

230 g (1/2 lb) of polyester stuffing

1 pair of safety eyes 8mm (5/16 in) in diameter

5 joints 2.5 cm (1 in) in diameter

45 cm (17 3/4 in) of 2.5 cm (1 in) wide ribbon for the neck

INSTRUCTIONS

1. Cut out all the pattern pieces from fabric

2. Stitch the gusset to the sides of the head, matching the rounded end to the nose and leaving a small opening on one of the back seams for inserting the joint and stuffing. Stitch from nose to neck

3. With right sides together, stitch around the curved edge of each ear, turn right side out and overstitch the straight edge

4. Stitch the ears to the head where indicated on the pattern piece and turn the head right side out

5. Attach the safety eyes where you feel they would look best and then embroider the nose and mouth

6. Stuff the head lightly, gather the neck edge and secure with a few stitches

7. With right sides together, pin and sew the two front sections of the body, creating a seam at the bear's centre front. Pin and stitch the front of the body to the two back sections and finally stitch the centre back seam leaving an opening for turning and stuffing. This will create four seams in total

8. Turn the body right side out and gather and secure the neck edge

9. Place a joint in the bear's head, push the shank into the body at the neck end and secure it with a washer. Finish stuffing the head very firmly to prevent it wobbling and oversew the opening

10. Stitch the paw pads to the forearms on the wrong side of the fabric. Pin and stitch the forearms to the back of the arms leaving a small opening on each for turning and stuffing

11. With right sides together, pin and stitch the leg seams leaving an opening at the back for turning and stuffing. Stitch the soles in place

12. Turn the legs and arms right side out

13. Attach the arms 5 cm (2 in) from the neck and the legs 5 cm (2 in) from the bottom of the body, securing the shanks of the joints inside the body with washers

14. Stuff the legs, arms and body (in that order) and oversew the openings

15. Tie a ribbon around Bertie's neck

AUGUSTUS

At 18 cm (7 in) high Georgie was so popular that I decided to make a similar sort of bear 5 cm (2 in) taller. The result was Augustus, who takes his name from the fact that he was actually designed in August. He can be made in smooth-pile fur fabric, felt, mohair or corduroy, but if you do use mohair it should be an especially short-pile one, which you may find difficult to obtain.

MATERIALS

33 cm (13 in) x 50 cm (19 3/4 in) of suitable fabric

small piece of brown felt or suede for paws and soles

length of black wool or embroidery cotton for nose and mouth

3 handfuls of polyester stuffing

1 pair of safety eyes 5 mm (1/4 in) in diameter

5 safety eyes 1 cm (3/8 in) in diameter (to use as joints)

45 cm (17 3/4 in) of 1 cm (3/8 in) wide ribbon

INSTRUCTIONS

1. Cut out all the pattern pieces in fabric

2. With right sides together, pin and stitch the gusset to the sides of the head matching the square end to the nose and leaving a small opening on one seam at the back of the head for inserting the joint and stuffing

3. Stitch from nose to neck

4. With right sides together, pin and stitch around the curved edge of each ear, turn right side out and overstitch the straight edge

5. Stitch the ears to the head and turn the head right side out

6. Embroider the nose and mouth

7. Stuff the head loosely, gather the neck edge and secure with a few stitches

8. Fold the pattern piece for each leg in two and, with right sides together, sew the seam leaving a small opening for turning and stuffing. Next stitch the soles in position

9. Sew the paw pads to the forearms and then, right sides together, pin and stitch the forearm to the back of each arm, again leaving a small opening for turning and stuffing

10. Turn the arms and legs right side out

11. With right sides together, pin and stitch the front seam of the body

12. Stitch the front of the body to the back leaving a small opening on one of the side seams for turning and stuffing

13. Turn the body right side out and gather the neck edge

14. Attach the head to the body, placing a safety eye as a joint in the neck. The shank should be secured with a washer inside the body. Finish stuffing the head very firmly and overstitch the opening at the back of the head

15. Using the safety eyes as joints, attach the arms 4 cm (1 1/2 in) from the neck, and the legs 4 cm (1 1/2 in) from the bottom of the body, securing the shanks inside the body with washers

16. Stuff the legs, arms and body in that order and overstitch the openings

17. To complete Augustus, tie a ribbon around his neck

WILLIAM

When I designed William I wanted him to look like a sailor bear, so he has a straw hat like those worn by the sailors in Nelson's navy and a black tie, which gives him a very smart appearance. William can move his arms but his legs are not jointed, so he always looks as though he is standing to attention. He is 30 cm (11 3/4 in) high.

MATERIALS

50 cm (19 3/4 in) short-pile fur fabric

small piece of felt for soles and paws

length of black wool or embroidery cotton for nose and mouth

230 g (1/2 lb) of polyester stuffing

1 pair of safety eyes 1 cm (3/8 in) in diameter

2 joints 2.5 cm (1 in) in diameter

45 cm (17 3/4 in) of 2.5 cm (1 in) wide black ribbon for the tie

straw hat with an opening 11.5 cm (4 1/2 in) in diameter (obtainable from dried flower shops)

1 m (39 1/2 in) of 1 cm (3/8 in) wide blue ribbon for trimming hat

50 cm (19 3/4 in) of narrow blue ribbon for holding hat on William's head

INSTRUCTIONS

1. Cut out all the pattern pieces in fabric after having attached the two sections of the gusset across A–B to enable you to cut it out as one complete piece

2. With wrong sides together, stitch the outer leg pieces to the straight edge at the bottom of the body. Then stitch the inner legs to the outer part of the legs leaving the top edge open. Stitch the soles into position

3. Carefully pin the gusset into position along one side starting with point C at the mouth and taking it under the chin, the widest part forming William's front. Then start pinning from point D, along nose, up and over the top of the head and down the bear's back. Ease the gussett between the legs for a neat fit

4. Repeat this process on the second side but leave an opening on the back seam for fixing the joints, turning and stuffing. Turn the body and legs right side out

5. Stitch the paw pads to the forearms on the wrong side of the fabric and follow by stitching the forearms to the back of the arms, leaving a small opening on one of the seams. Turn the arms right side out

6. Using the joints, attach the arms to the body 2.5 cm (1 in) from the neck.

The shanks of the joints should be secured inside the body with washers. Stuff the arms firmly and oversew the openings

7. Attach the safety eyes when you have found the most suitable expression for the bear and then embroider the nose and mouth

8. With right sides together, stitch round the curved edge of the ears leaving the inner edge open. Turn them right side out and overstitch the opening. Make small cuts in the head to accommodate the ears and stitch them in position leaving 5 cm (2 in) between them at the top of the head

9. Stuff the bear very firmly through the opening at the back of the body, making sure that the neck is very firmly stuffed to prevent the head from wobbling. Overstitch the opening

10. Trim the brim edge of the hat with blue ribbon and tie the remaining ribbon round the crown. Attach a narrower length of ribbon to the hat which can be tied under William's chin

11. Form a tie round William's neck with the black ribbon

JOHNNIE

By now you will probably have had enough practice to start creating some of your own bears from the different pattern pieces in this book. I thought a morris-dancing bear would be an attractive addition to the collection and decided to make Johnnie using Septimus's head, Edward's shapely body as well as his legs, which are long and slender, and Timothy's arms, which have a graceful look just right for waving handkerchiefs.

MATERIALS

45 cm (17 3/4 in) of distressed mohair or medium-pile fur fabric

piece of brown felt for soles and paws

length of black wool or embroidery cotton for nose and mouth

115 g (1/4 lb) of polyester stuffing

1 pair of safety eyes 1 cm (3/8 in) in diameter

5 joints 5 cm (2 in) in diameter

46 cm (18 1/8 in) of 2.5 cm (1 in) wide ribbon

5 small bells

straw hat 20 cm (8 in) in diameter with a brim (obtainable from dried flower shops)

15 cm (6 in) of narrow elastic to secure hat to head

oddments of coloured felt to make flowers for trimming hat

INSTRUCTIONS

1. Cut out the pattern pieces in fabric for Edward's body and legs, Septimus' head and Timothy's arms

2. Pin and stitch the pieces together following the instructions given for the bears from which the patterns are taken

3. Cut out flower shapes from the felt to trim the hat and attach three bells to the brim

4. Stitch elastic to the hat to hold it on Johnnie's head

5. Sew a bell to each end of the ribbon and tie it round the bear's neck

MᴄCᴀʀᴛʜʏ

 *I was recently privileged to meet John McCarthy and Jill Morrell and was so impressed by their dignity and charm that I wanted to create a bear as a tribute to them. I decided to make a bear 33 cm (13 in) tall and, after long consideration, chose to use Henry's head, Timothy's legs and body, and Edward's arms. I was delighted with the end result.*

The choice of material is up to you. I chose a smooth-pile, silky fur fabric in a soft-mink colour. The crucial thing to remember is that the ribbon around the bear's neck must be yellow, as yellow ribbons were adopted as a symbol of freedom while John McCarthy was in captivity. I used wool felt for his paws and feet because it is softer than ordinary felt, and embroidered his nose in black mercerised cotton which also gave it a softer appearance.

To sew each pattern piece, refer to the instructions for the bear from which you have taken it and, when complete, you will have a unique bear to honour a unique couple.

TIMOTHY

I made Timothy for a friend of mine who, as a child, had never been given a bear. Occasionally when I design a bear he turns out better than I ever could have hoped and Timothy is one of those bears. His sharp little nose gives him an inquisitive air - so much so that his new owner sometimes thinks of taking him from room to room so that he can observe all the activities going on in the house. Timothy is based on a pattern from 1955 and measures 33 cm (13 in) high.

MATERIALS

25 cm (9 3/4 in) of long-pile fur fabric, distressed mohair or loom-state fur fabric

small piece of felt or suede for paws and soles

length of black wool or embroidery cotton for nose and mouth

340 g (12 oz) of polyester stuffing

1 pair of safety eyes 1 cm (3/8 in) in diameter

5 joints 2.5 cm (1 in) in diameter

75 cm (29 1/2 in) of 4 cm (1 1/2 in) wide ribbon

INSTRUCTIONS

1. Cut out all the pattern pieces from fabric. When cutting the arms, refer to the instructions for cutting out Nathaniel's arms on page 62

2. Stitch the head gusset to the sides of the head, matching the rounded end to the nose and leaving an opening on one back seam to allow for inserting the joint and stuffing. Then stitch from nose to neck

3. With right sides together, stitch around the curved edge of each ear, turn right side out and oversew the inner edge

4. Stitch the ears into the head as indicated on the pattern piece and turn the head right side out

5. Fasten the safety eyes in your preferred position and then embroider the nose and mouth

6. Stuff the head lightly. Gather the neck edge and secure with a few stitches

7. Stitch the paw pads to the forearms on the wrong side of the fabric and then stitch each forearm to the back of the arms leaving a small opening on the back seam for stuffing and turning

8. With right sides together, stitch the leg seams, again leaving an opening on the back seam for turning and stuffing. Stitch the soles into position

9. Turn the legs and arms right side out

10. With right sides together, pin and stitch the body gusset to the two side body pieces. Stitch the back seam leaving an opening for fixing the joints and stuffing. Turn the body right side out and gather the neck edge

11. Attach the head to the body using a joint, pushing the shank through the neck and securing it inside the body with a washer. Finish stuffing the head firmly and oversew the opening

12. Using the joints and pushing the shanks into the body, fasten the arms 5 cm (2 in) from the neck and the legs 5 cm (2 in) from the bottom of the body

13. Stuff the legs, arms and body (in that order) and overstitch the openings. If you have used fur fabric, brush the seams with a teasel brush to hide them, but you should not do this if you have used loom-state fabric

14. Tie a ribbon round Timothy's neck

ALBERT

Albert was designed especially for Granada television's This Morning *in December 1991 and named after the Albert Docks where the programme is recorded. He was made in traditional honey-coloured, short-pile fur fabric and designed in the style of a 1962 bear with shorter arms and legs than many others in this book. He stands 40.5 cm (16 in) tall and, to make him that little bit different, Albert has tweed paws and feet although suede or felt would do just as well. He must wear a blue ribbon to represent the colour of the water around the* This Morning *studios.*

MATERIALS

51 cm (20 in) of honey-coloured, short-pile fur fabric

piece of tweed, felt or suede for the paws and soles

length of wool or embroidery cotton for nose and mouth

455 g (1 lb) of polyester stuffing

1 pair of safety eyes 1 cm (3/8 in) in diameter

5 joints 2.5 cm (1 in) in diameter

70 cm (27 1/2 in) of 5 cm (2 in) wide deep-blue ribbon

INSTRUCTIONS

1. Cut out all the pattern pieces in fabric as instructed. When cutting out the legs, remember to double the fabric and position the fold line of the paper pattern piece against the fold in the fabric

2. With right sides together, stitch the gusset to the head pieces matching the rounded end to the nose and leaving an opening at the back of the head for inserting the joint and stuffing

3. Stitch from nose to neck

4. With right sides together, stitch around the curved edge of each ear, turn right side out and overstitch the straight edge

5. Stitch the ears into the head in the position shown on the pattern piece

6. Turn the head right side out. Position the safety eyes and embroider the nose and mouth

7. Stuff the head lightly, gather the neck edge and secure

8. Stitch the paws to the forearms on the wrong side of the fabric. Then sew the forearms to the back of the arms leaving a small opening on the back seam for turning and stuffing. Turn the arms right side out

9. Fold the legs in half, right sides together, and stitch the seam leaving a small opening for turning and stuffing

10. Stitch the soles in position and turn the legs right side out

11. Stitch the darts on the two body sections. With right sides together, pin and stitch the body pieces leaving an opening on the back seam for fixing the joints and stuffing

12. Turn the body right side out and gather the neck edge

13. Place a joint inside the head and push the shank through into the neck of the body, securing it with a washer. Finish stuffing the head firmly and overstitch the opening at the back

14. Place joints in the arms, attaching them to the body 6 cm (2 3/8 in) from the neck. Attach the legs 6 cm (3/8 in) from the bottom of the body. Push the shanks of the joints into the body and fix them in place with washers

15. Stuff the legs, arms and body in that order and overstitch the openings

16. Tie a blue ribbon around Albert's neck

HENRY

Henry is designed in the style of a 1920s bear, with upstanding ears, wide-apart eyes and big feet - the sign of all good bears. The original model for Henry is very blond, so I made him from short-pile distressed blond mohair. He is 36-38 cm (14-15 in) tall.

MATERIALS

50 cm (29 3/4 in) of blond fur fabric or short-pile distressed mohair

small piece of felt or suede for paws and soles

length of black wool or embroidery cotton for nose and mouth

455 g (1 lb) of polyester stuffing

1 pair of safety eyes 1 cm (3/8 in) in diameter

5 joints 2.5 cm (1 in) in diameter

28 cm (11 in) of 4 cm (5/8 in) wide ribbon

INSTRUCTIONS

1. Cut out all the pattern pieces in fabric. When cutting out the legs, double the fabric and place the fold line of the paper pattern piece against the fold in the fabric

2. Stitch the gusset to the head pieces matching the square end to the nose and leaving an opening on one of the back seams for turning, inserting the joint and stuffing

3. Stitch round the curved edge of each ear on the wrong side of the fabric. Turn the ears right side and overstitch the straight edge

4. Stitch the ears into position on the head

5. Turn the head right side out, attach the safety eyes and embroider the nose and mouth. Stuff the head lightly and gather the neck edge

6. Sew the paws to the forearms on the wrong side of the fabric. Pin the forearms to the back of the arms and stitch together leaving an opening for turning and stuffing. Turn the arms right side out

7. With right sides together, sew the seam for each leg leaving an opening for turning and stuffing

8. Stitch the soles in position and turn the legs right side out

9. With right sides together, stitch the two front sections of the body

10. Stitch the front of the body to the back leaving an opening on one of the side seams for turning and stuffing. Turn the body right side out and gather the neck edge

11. Attach the head to the body, pushing the shank of the joint through the neck and securing it with a washer inside the body. Finish stuffing the head firmly and oversew the opening at the back

12. Attach the arms and legs to the body, measuring 5 cm (2 in) from the neck for the arms and the same from the bottom of the body for the legs

13. Stuff the legs, arms and body in that order and overstitch the openings in the seams

14. Tie a ribbon around Henry's neck

MARMADUKE

 *Marmaduke is 43 cm (17 in) high and was designed specially for a friend suffering from multiple sclerosis. Bears can be a great comfort, particularly to those in need of a friend. Some time ago, I made one for a six-year-old granddaughter staying in hospital, away from her mother for the first time. I told her that he would lend a sympathetic ear when she felt alone at night. When she eventually came home, she thought he was a magical bear who had granted her wish to be made better! Marmaduke does not claim to cure ills, but he always gives comfort where it is most needed.*

MATERIALS

25 cm (9 3/4 in) of long-pile mohair or fur fabric

5 cm (2 in) x 40 cm (15 3/4 in) felt or suede for paws and soles

length of black wool or embroidery cotton for nose and mouth

455 g (1 lb) of polyester stuffing

1 pair of safety eyes 1 cm (3/8 in) in diameter

5 joints 4.5 cm (1 3/4 in) in diameter

90 cm (35 1/2 in) of 5 cm (2 in) wide ribbon

INSTRUCTIONS

1. Cut out all the pattern pieces in fabric

2. With right sides together, pin and stitch the gusset to the two head pieces matching the rounded end to the nose and leaving about 5 cm (2 in) open on one back seam for inserting the joint and stuffing. Stitch from nose to neck

3. Stitch round the curved edge of the ears on the wrong side of the fabric. Turn the ears right side out and overstitch the straight edge

4. Attach the ears to the head as indicated on the pattern piece and turn the head right side out

5. Attach the safety eyes in the position marked on the pattern piece. Then embroider the nose and mouth and trim the snout

6. Stuff the head lightly and gather the neck edge

7. Stitch the paws to the forearms and then, right sides together, stitch the forearms to the back of the arms leaving a small opening for turning and stuffing

8. With right sides together, pin and stitch the leg sections leaving a small opening for fixing the joints and stuffing

9. Turn the arms and legs right side out

10. Stitch the front body seam and then the back, leaving an opening at the back for turning and stuffing

11. Turn the body right side out and gather the neck edge

12. Attach the head to the body, fixing the shank securely inside the neck of the body with a washer. Finish stuffing the head firmly and oversew the opening at the back

13. Push joints into the legs and attach them 5 cm (2 in) from the bottom of the body. Push joints into the arms and attach them to the body 5 cm (2 in) from the neck. Secure the shanks of the joints inside the body with washers

14. Stuff the legs, arms and body, in that order, very firmly. You may wish to use the handle of a wooden spoon to push small pieces of stuffing into place. Oversew the openings

15. Brush the seams with a teasel brush to conceal the stitching

16. Tie a ribbon around Marmaduke's neck

EDWARD

Edward is designed in the style of one of the very earliest bears from around 1903. He is 36 cm (14 1/8 in) high with a long snout and a wide forehead. He looks just right in smooth fur fabric or distressed mohair, which are the modern equivalents of the types of material used in the early twentieth century.

MATERIALS

30 cm (11 3/4 in) of smooth fur fabric or distressed mohair

small piece of felt or suede for paws and soles

length of black wool or embroidery cotton for nose and mouth

455 g (1 lb) of polyester stuffing

1 pair of safety eyes 1 cm (3/8 in) in diameter

5 joints 2.5 cm (1 in) in diameter

68 cm (26 3/4 in) of 4 cm (1 5/8 in) wide ribbon

INSTRUCTIONS

1. Cut out all the pattern pieces in fabric. When cutting out the legs, double the fabric and position the fold line on the paper pattern piece up against the fold in the fabric

2. With right sides together, stitch the gusset to the head pieces matching the rounded end to the nose and leaving an opening at the back for inserting the joint and stuffing. Stitch from nose to neck

3. Stitch around the curved edge of each ear on the wrong side of the fabric, turn right side out and overstitch the straight edge

4. Stitch the ears into the head as marked on the pattern piece

5. Turn the head right side out and fasten the safety eyes in place. Embroider the nose and mouth. Stuff the head lightly and gather the neck edge

6. Fold the legs in half and, right sides together, sew the front seam remembering to leave an opening for turning and stuffing. Stitch the soles in position and turn the legs right side out

7. Stitch a paw to each forearm, then stitch the forearms to the back of the arms leaving an opening on the back seam for turning and stuffing

8. With right sides together, pin and stitch the two front sections of the body at centre front. Stitch the side seams, attaching the front of the body to the two back sections. Stitch the centre back seam leaving an opening for fixing the joints and stuffing

9. Turn the body right side out and gather the neck edge

10. Attach the head to the body, placing a joint through the neck and securing it in the body with a washer. Finish stuffing the head firmly and oversew the back opening

11. Fasten the arms to the body 5 cm (2 in) from the neck and the legs 5 cm (2 in) from the bottom of the body. Secure the shanks inside the body with washers

12. Stuff the legs, arms and body firmly and oversew all the openings

13. Brush the seams with a teasel brush to conceal them and tie a ribbon around Edward's neck

RUBEN

I liked the two names Rupert and Benjamin and decided to put them together to form the name Ruben. It seemed very appropriate for this bear who I think of as being a bit of an artist. Ruben is designed in the style of a 1940s bear and is 41 cm (16 in) high.

MATERIALS

50 cm (19 3/4 in) of mohair or long-pile fur fabric

small piece of brown felt for paws and soles

length of black wool or embroidery cotton for nose and mouth

455 g (1 lb) of polyester stuffing

1 pair of safety eyes 1 cm (3/8 in) in diameter

5 joints 4.5 cm (1 3/4 in) in diameter

70 cm (27 1/2 in) of 5 cm (2 in) wide ribbon

INSTRUCTIONS

1. Cut out all the pattern pieces in fabric

2. With right sides together, stitch the gusset to the two front pieces of the head matching the rounded end to the nose

3. With right sides together, stitch round the curved edge of the ears, turn them right side out and overstitch the straight edge

4. Pin the edge of the gusset to the back section of the head and stitch together for 5 cm (2 in) along the top. Then stitch the ears in position on either side before continuing to stitch the rest of the front of the head to the back. Leave a small opening for inserting the joint and stuffing

5. Stitch from nose to neck and turn the head right side out

6. Attach the safety eyes and embroider the nose and mouth

7. Stuff the head lightly. Gather the neck edge and secure

8. With right sides together, stitch the seam on each leg leaving a small opening for turning and stuffing

9. Stitch the soles in position and turn the legs right side out

10. Stitch the paws to the forearms on the wrong side of the fabric. With right sides together, pin and stitch the forearms to the back of the arms leaving an opening. Turn the arms right side out

11. With right sides together, pin and stitch the two front sections of the body forming a seam at centre front

12. Stitch the side seams to attach the front of the body to the two back sections. Then stitch the seam at centre back leaving an opening for turning and stuffing

13. Turn the body right side out and gather the neck edge. Attach the head to the body, placing a joint through the neck and fixing the shank inside the body with a washer

14. Finish stuffing the head and oversew the opening at the back

15. Attach the arms to the body 6 cm (2 3/8 in) from the neck and the legs 6 cm (2 3/8 in) from the bottom of the body. Push the shanks of the joints inside the body and secure them with washers

16. Stuff the legs, arms and body (in that order) and overstitch the openings

17. Tie a ribbon around Ruben's neck

SEPTIMUS

The reason for this bear's name is that he was designed in September for a special birthday. Made in distressed mohair, he has the characteristics of a 1930s bear with slender arms, big feet and a beguiling face. Septimus is 36 cm (14 in) high.

MATERIALS

25 cm (9 3/4 in) of distressed mohair or long-pile fur fabric

small piece of brown suede or felt for paws and soles

length of black wool or embroidery cotton for nose and mouth

400 g (14 oz) of polyester stuffing

1 pair of safety eyes 5 mm (1/4 in) in diameter

5 joints 3.5 cm (1 3/8 in) in length

45 cm (17 3/4 in) of 4 cm (1 5/8 in) wide ribbon

INSTRUCTIONS

1. Cut out all the pattern pieces in fabric. When cutting out the legs, remember to double the fabric and place the fold line of the paper pattern piece against the fold in the fabric

2. With right sides together, stitch the gusset to the sides of the head matching the rounded end to the nose and leaving an opening on one back seam for inserting the joint and stuffing. Stitch from nose to neck

3. With right sides together, stitch round the curved edge of the ears, turn them right side out and oversew the inner edge

4. Attach the ears to the head as indicated on the pattern piece and turn the head right side out

5. Attach the safety eyes as marked on the pattern piece and embroider the nose and mouth. Stuff the head lightly, gather the neck edge and secure

6. Stitch the paws to the forearms on the wrong side of the fabric. With right sides together, stitch the forearms to the back of the arms leaving an opening on the back seam for turning and stuffing

7. With right sides together, stitch the seam on each leg leaving an opening for turning and stuffing

8. Stitch the soles into position and turn the legs right side out

9. Stitch the darts at the top and bottom of each body section

10. With right sides together, stitch the front body seam and then the back seam leaving a small opening for turning and stuffing

11. Turn the body right side out, gather the neck and secure. Attach the head to the body, pushing a joint through the neck and fixing the shank inside the body with a washer

12. Finish stuffing the head and oversew the opening at the back

13. Attach the arms to the body 5 cm (2 in) from the neck. Attach the legs on each side 2.5 cm (1 in) from the bottom of the body. Secure the shanks of the joints inside the body

14. Stuff the legs, arms and body (in that order) and oversew the openings

15. Brush all the oversewn seams with a teasel brush to conceal them

16. Tie a ribbon around the bear's neck

ANNIVERSARY

I designed this very special bear as a gift to celebrate a fiftieth wedding anniversary. Unlike china or glass, a bear is both unbreakable and original. Anniversary is 40 cm (15 3/4 in) high and is designed in the style of a 1930s bear with an appealing face and compact body.

MATERIALS

25 cm (9 3/4 in) of long-pile mohair or fur fabric

7 cm (2 3/4 in) x 35 cm (13 3/4 in) suede or felt for paws and soles

length of black wool or embroidery cotton for nose and mouth

455 g (1 lb) of polyester stuffing

1 pair of safety eyes 5 mm (1/4 in) in diameter

5 joints 4.5 cm (1 3/4 in) in diameter

68 cm (26 3/4 in) of 5 cm (2 in) wide ribbon

INSTRUCTIONS

1. Cut out all the pattern pieces in fabric

2. Stitch the gusset to the two head pieces, matching the rounded end to the nose and leaving an opening on one back seam for inserting the joint and stuffing. Sew from nose to neck

3. With right sides together, stitch round the curved edge of the ears, turn them right side out and oversew the straight edge

4. Stitch the ears in position as marked on the pattern piece and turn the head right side out

5. Attach the safety eyes, embroider the nose and mouth and trim the muzzle. Stuff the head lightly and gather the neck edge

6. Stitch the paws to the forearms on the wrong side of the fabric. With right sides together, stitch the forearms to the back of the arms leaving an opening on the back seam. Turn the arms right side out

7. With right sides together, stitch the seam on each leg leaving a small opening for turning and stuffing

8. Stitch the soles into position and turn the legs right side out

9. Stich the darts at the top and bottom of each body section and, with right sides together, pin and stitch the two pieces together. Leave a small opening on the back seam for attaching the joints and stuffing

10. Turn the body right side out and gather the neck edge. Attach the head, pushing a joint through into the neck and securing the shank inside the body with a washer

11. Finish stuffing the head and oversew the opening at the back

12. Attach the arms to the body 2.5 cm (1 in) from the neck and the legs 2.5 cm (1 in) from the bottom of the body

13. Stuff the legs, arms and body (in that order) very firmly, using the handle of a wooden spoon to push small pieces of stuffing into position if you find it helps. Oversew the openings

14. Brush the oversewn seams with a teasel brush to hide the stitching

15. Tie a ribbon round Anniversary's neck

NATHANIEL

Nathaniel is a broad-faced bear similar to the type made just before the Second World War. He is 43 cm (17 in) tall and his body is well shaped with a slightly humped back. He should be made in long-pile fur fabric or, better still, distressed mohair.

MATERIALS

50 cm (19 3/4 in) of distressed mohair or long-pile fur fabric

small square of brown felt for paws and soles

length of black wool or embroidery cotton for nose and mouth

455 g (1 lb) of polyester stuffing

1 pair of safety eyes 1 cm (3/8 in) in diameter

5 joints 4.5 cm (1 3/4 in) in diameter

68 cm (26 3/4 in) of 7.5 cm (3 in) wide ribbon for neck

INSTRUCTIONS

1. Cut out the pattern pieces in fabric. The back of each arm is cut as one complete piece but the forearms and paws are cut as separate pieces. Add an extra 5 mm (1/4 in) in length at the straight end of the paw to allow for joining it to the forearm

2. With right sides together, stitch the gusset to the sides of the head matching the wider square end to the nose and leaving an opening at the back for inserting the joint and stuffing. Stitch from nose to neck

3. With right sides together, stitch round the curved edge of the ears, turn them right side out and overstitch the straight edge

4. Stitch the ears in place as marked on the pattern and turn the head right side out

5. Attach the safety eyes and embroider the nose and mouth. Stuff the head lightly, gather the neck edge and secure

6. Stitch the paws to the forearms on the wrong side of the fabric. Then stitch the forearms to the back of the arms leaving an opening on one seam. Turn the arms right side out

7. With right sides together, pin and stitch the leg seams leaving an opening at the back for turning and stuffing

8. Stitch the soles in position and turn the legs right side out

9. With right sides together, stitch the front body seam. Then stitch the two side seams joining the front to the two back sections. Stitch the centre back seam leaving a small opening for fixing the joints and stuffing

10. Turn the body right side out and gather the neck edge. Attach the head, placing a joint through the neck and securing the shank inside the body

11. Finish stuffing the head and oversew the opening at the back

12. Attach the arms 6 cm (2 3/8 in) from the neck and the legs 6 cm (2 3/8 in) from the bottom of the body. Secure the shanks of the joints inside the body with washers

13. Stuff the legs, arms and body (in that order) and oversew the openings

14. Tie a ribbon round Nathaniel's neck

DAVID

David is a little more difficult to make than some of the other bears in the book because his muzzle must be cut and stitched separately. He is designed in the style of a 1930s bear with extra-large feet, and was first made on Saint David's Day. David stands 51 cm (20 in) high.

MATERIALS

70 cm (27 1/2 in) long-pile fur fabric or distressed mohair

22 cm (8 5/8 in) square of brown felt for paws and soles

small piece of smooth-pile fur fabric, mohair or velvet for snout

length of black wool or embroidery cotton for nose and mouth

910 g (2 lbs) of polyester stuffing

1 pair of safety eyes 8 mm (3/8 in) in diameter

5 joints 5 cm (2 in) in diameter

46 cm (18 1/8 in) red ribbon

INSTRUCTIONS

1. Cut out all the pattern pieces in fabric. For this bear, a seam width of 1 cm (3/8 in) has been allowed for and 2 cm (3/4 in) for the muzzle. When cutting out the arms, refer to the instructions for cutting out Nathaniel's arms on page 62

2. With right sides together, stitch the gusset to the sides of the head. Match the narrower, curved edge to the front (where the muzzle will be joined to the face) and the wide edge to the point at the top of each side piece

3. Fold the muzzle in half with right sides together and stitch the outer curved edge. With the seam pointing down towards the chin, stitch the muzzle into the space between the two side pieces and the gusset. Stitch from underneath the muzzle to the neck

4. With right sides together, stitch round the curved edge of the ears, turn them right side out and overstitch the inner edge

5. Starting where the gusset and face side join at the top of the head, pin and stitch each ear in place

6. Pin and stitch the back sections of the head to the sides. The wider, curved end of each piece forms the neck edge and the pointed ends join the top of the gusset. Stitch part of the seam at centre back of the head leaving an opening for inserting the joint and stuffing

7. Turn the head right side out and attach the safety eyes to the face sides 1 cm (3/8 in) down from the gusset seam. Embroider the nose and mouth. Stuff the head lightly and gather the neck edge

8. Stitch the paws to the forearms on the wrong side of the fabric. With right sides together, stitch the forearms to the back of the arms leaving an opening on the back seam. Turn the arms right side out

9. With right sides together, join the leg pieces leaving an opening at the back. Stitch in the soles and turn the legs right side out

10. With right sides together, join the two front sections of the body. Pin the front of the body to the back sections at the sides and stitch them together. Stitch the centre back seam leaving an opening for fixing the joints and stuffing

11. Turn the body right side out and gather the neck edge. Attach the head, placing the joint through the neck. Finish stuffing the head and oversew the opening at the back

12. Attach the arms to the body 6 cm (2 3/8 in) from the neck. Attach the legs 6 cm (3/8 in) from the bottom of the body. Secure the shanks inside the body with washers

13. Stuff the legs, arms and body and oversew the openings

14. Tie a ribbon round David's neck

ROB ROY

Rob Roy is a sturdy bear with plenty of character. He stands 38 cm (15 in) high and is designed in the style of a 1925 bear with long, slender arms and feet and a humped back. His paws and the soles of his feet are in Rob Roy tartan to match his tam-o'-shanter, and his ribbon is in MacGregor tartan. He is best made in distressed mohair or long-pile fur fabric.

MATERIALS

50 cm (19 3/4 in) distressed mohair or long-pile fur fabric

25 cm (9 3/4 in) Rob Roy tartan material (black and red checks) for paws, soles and hat

length of black wool or embroidery cotton for nose and mouth

455 g (1 lb) of polyester stuffing

1 pair of safety eyes 1 cm (3/8 in) in diameter

5 joints 5 cm (2 in) in diameter

50 cm (19 3/4 in) of 3.5 cm (1 3/8 in) wide MacGregor tartan ribbon

small ball of red double knitting wool (to match the Rob Roy tartan) for the pompon

22 cm (8 5/8 in) of narrow elastic to secure hat to head

INSTRUCTIONS

1. Cut out all the pattern pieces in fabric. When cutting out the arms, refer to the instructions for cutting out Nathaniel's arms on page 62

2. Stitch the gusset to the sides of the head, matching the narrow rounded end to the nose and leaving an opening on one back seam for inserting the joint and stuffing. Stitch from nose to neck

3. With right sides together, pin and stitch round the curved edge of the ears and turn them right side out. Oversew the straight edge of each ear and stitch them to the head as marked on the pattern piece

4. Turn the head right side out and attach the safety eyes. Embroider the nose and mouth. Stuff the head lightly and gather the neck edge

5. Stitch the paws to the forearms on the wrong side of the fabric. Then, with right sides together, stitch the forearms to the back of the arms leaving an opening. Turn the arms right side out

6. With right sides together, stitch the leg seams leaving an opening at the back for turning and stuffing

7. Stitch the soles of the feet in place and turn the legs right side out

8. With right sides together, join the two front sections of the body. Pin and stitch the side seams. Then stitch the seam at centre back leaving an opening for fixing the joints and stuffing the bear

9. Turn the body right side out and gather the neck edge. Attach the head, placing a joint through the neck and securing the shank inside the body with a washer

10. Finish stuffing the head and oversew the opening at the back

11. Attach the arms to the body 6 cm (2 3/8 in) from the neck. Attach the legs 6 cm (2 3/8 in) from the bottom of the body. Secure the shanks of the joints inside the body with washers

12. Stuff the legs, arms and body (in that order) and oversew the openings

13. Tie the MacGregor tartan ribbon round Rob Roy's neck

TAM-O'-SHANTER

1. Cut two circles of Rob Roy tartan 20 cm (8 in) in diameter

2. Place the circles on top of each other with right sides together and stitch round the circumference 5 mm (1/4 in) in from the edge

3. Insert the point of your scissors in the centre of one circle and cut an inner circle 4 cm (1 5/8 in) in diameter

4. Make several small cuts 5 mm (1/4 in) in length radiating from the edge of the inner circle to enable you to turn the rough edge in by the same amount (5 mm (1/4 in)). Sew this hem using herring-bone stitch. Follow the instructions on page 14 for the pompon

RAMSAY

Named after the tartan he wears, I designed Ramsay using the patterns for some of the other bears of a similar size in the book. I felt that playing the bagpipes would demand great concentration and so chose Septimus' head, which has a very wise and intelligent look to it. I used Timothy's body, which is slim, suggesting an energetic, outdoor type of bear, and Edward's limbs. Ramsay is 38cm (15in) tall.

MATERIALS

46 cm (18 1/8 in) mohair or fur fabric of your choice

small piece of felt or suede for paws and soles

length of black wool or embroidery cotton for nose and mouth

455 g (1 lb) of polyester stuffing

1 pair of safety eyes 1 cm (3/8 in) in diameter

5 joints 4.5 cm (1 3/4 in) in diameter

blue and white wool (to match the Ramsay tartan) for the pompon and the bagpipe cord

46 cm (18 1/8 in) of 5 cm (2 in) wide ribbon for neck

dowel rod 30 cm (11 3/4 in) long and 5 mm (1/4 in) in diameter or use 5 varnished wooden lace bobbins

35 cm (13 3/4 in) x 25 cm (9 3/4 in) of Ramsay tartan for cap and bagpipes

white and black paint

INSTRUCTIONS

1. Cut out Septimus' head, Timothy's body and Edward's arms and legs in fabric

2. Pin and stitch the pieces together following the instructions given for the bears from which the patterns are taken

3. Stuff the bear and oversew the openings

4. Tie the ribbon round Ramsay's neck

BAGPIPES

1. If you are using a dowel rod, cut it into five lengths to make the pipes: chanter 5 cm (2 in), blowpipe 5 cm (2 in), bass drone 10 cm (4 in), 2 tenor drones 5 cm (2 in). Smooth the ends of the rods with sandpaper and paint each one black

2. Paint a white band 2 mm (1/8 in) wide round one end of the chanter and the blowpipe. Paint three white bands equal distances apart on the bass drone and two white bands on the tenor drones

3. Cut a 15 cm square of Ramsay tartan and fold it into a rectangle 15 cm (6 in) x 7.5 cm (3 in) to make the bag. With right sides together, stitch the cloth into a bag shape, as seen in the photograph and illustration, leaving a small opening for turning and stuffing. Turn the bag right side out and stuff lightly. Oversew the opening

4. Arrange the pipes as shown in the diagram, making small holes in the fabric with the point of a pair of sharp scissors and pushing the ends of the pipes inside the bag. Put a dab of glue on the end of each rod and squeeze the fabric tightly round it to hold it in place

5. Plait three strands of wool 25 cm (9 3/4 in) long which match the colour of the tartan. Knot the wool just before you reach the end and separate the strands to form a tassel. Wind the plaited wool round the pipes and attach as shown in the illustration

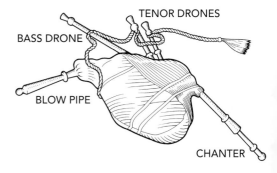

TAM-O'-SHANTER

Follow exactly the same instructions as for Rob Roy's tam-o'-shanter and the instructions for making a pompon (see page 14) but use Ramsay tartan

Suggestions for other bears

There is no limit to the number of different bears you can make by using a variety of fabrics and mixing the pattern pieces. But do remember when choosing heads and limbs to check that they come from bears of the same size or you will end up with something completely out of proportion. The main advantage of using material without a pile is that it is much easier to control on a sewing machine.

MAKE SURE that the material you use is sturdy enough to take stuffing without losing its shape and, as with fur fabrics, it must comply with EC safety regulations if you are offering the bear for sale. I have made a couple of bears in both corduroy and material without a pile to demonstrate how the shape and size of the bear is affected in each case.

If you use fabric without a pile, the features become sharper, the overall size of the bear smaller. Compare the plaid Timothy (right) with the one made in fur fabric (page 47), and similarly the corduroy Bertie (page 71) with the fur one (page 37). The choice of plain or patterned material will also affect the appearance of the bear.

MAKING BEARS TO SELL

New Regulations: European safety standards for toy-making have recently become much more stringent. The essential safety requirements are that anyone who handles the toy must be protected against health and injury risks when the toy is used reasonably. There must be no sharp edges, no easily removable

components that could be swallowed, and the fabric must not easily ignite when near a flame. Always buy good quality polyester stuffing from a reputable supplier because this too must not be inflammable. At the point of sale, toys must carry a label identifying the maker and showing a CE mark. The CE mark guarantees that the toy fully meets the requirements of Safety Standard BS 5665. This is a regulation relating to the supply of toys for children under 14. A toy-maker who wishes to use a CE label has two choices; either to send their toys to an approved testing house or, self-certification. To comply with BS 5665 by means of self-certification, a toy-maker must be able to guarantee that there is nothing inherent in his/her fabrics, felt, toy components (when fitted correctly!) or fillings that should cause toys made in a sensible way to fail BS 5665.

WHAT TO DO

Make sure you keep receipts, records of fabrics used etc., from your suppliers for all materials and components. Always use branded cotton for sewing up and, as a general guideline, 10-12 stitches per 2.5 cm (1 in) is recommended. Eyes and noses must be embedded in such a way that they cannot be gripped by a child's teeth or fingers. If they can be gripped, they must be able to withstand a weight of 9.2 kg (20.2 lb) for 10 seconds. By putting a washer on straight and firm you can be confident that these requirements will be met. If the toy has sharp edges or any other feature that you consider may be hazardous to a small child, it should be marked 'unsuitable for children under 3 years'.

Pattern pieces

The pattern pieces for the bears appear on the following pages. Each one can be traced straight from the page or you can photocopy the patterns which will save you some time. The arrows indicate the direction of the pile on the fabric. A narrow seam width has been allowed for on each pattern piece. Before cutting out a set of patterns, it is very important that you read all the way through the instructions for the bear you have chosen to make and refer also to the Before you begin section on pages 11-15.

CHRISTABEL

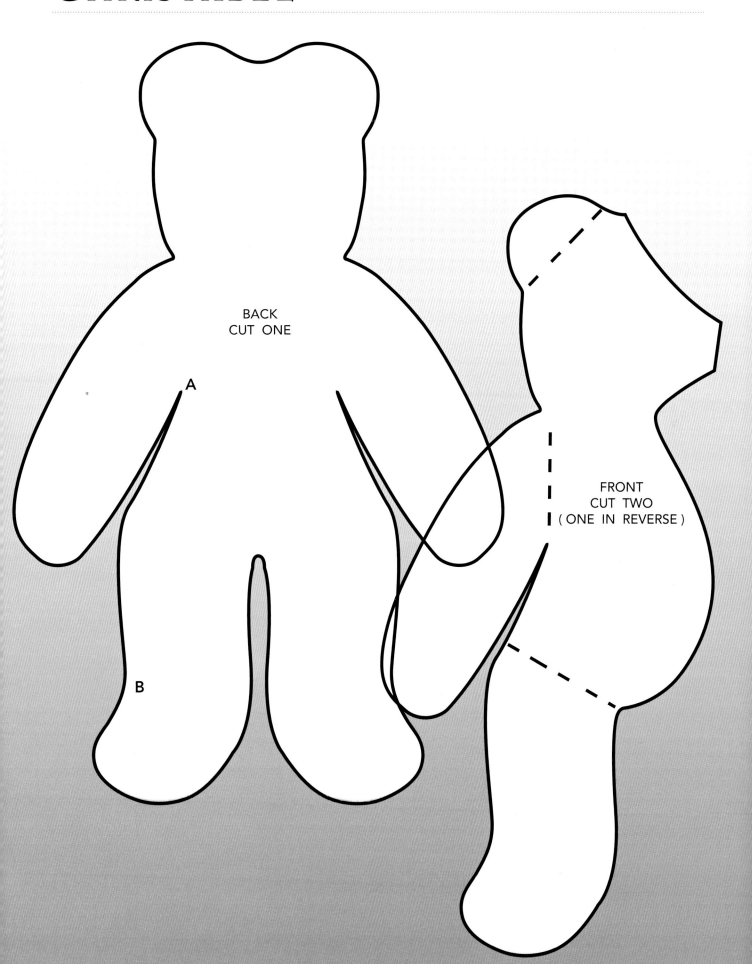

BACK
CUT ONE

A

B

FRONT
CUT TWO
(ONE IN REVERSE)

Holly

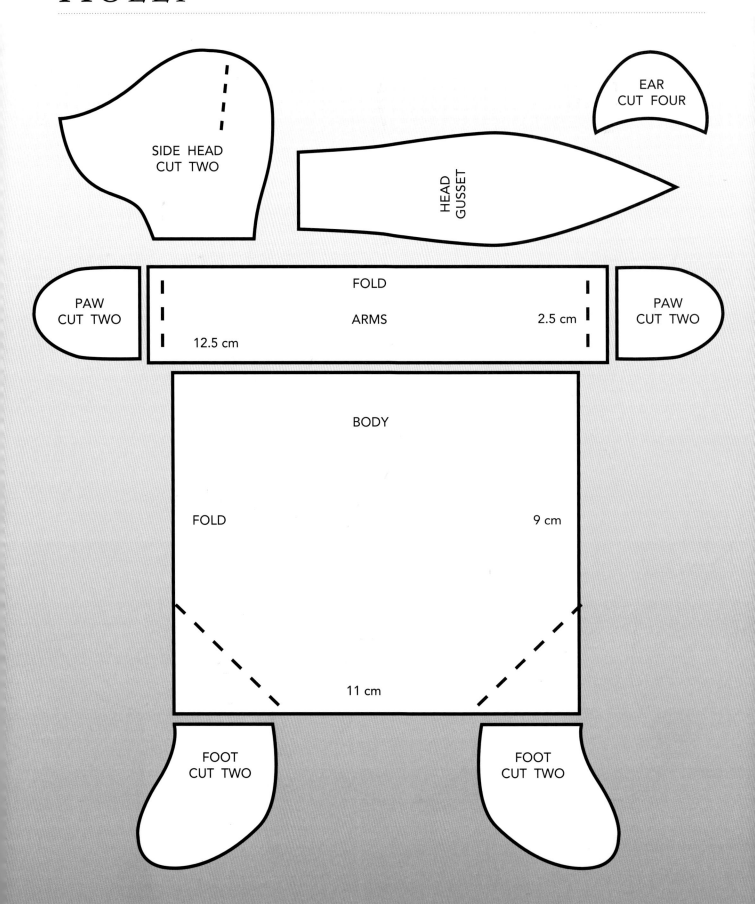

SIDE HEAD
CUT TWO

HEAD
GUSSET

EAR
CUT FOUR

PAW
CUT TWO

FOLD

ARMS

2.5 cm

12.5 cm

PAW
CUT TWO

BODY

FOLD

9 cm

11 cm

FOOT
CUT TWO

FOOT
CUT TWO

NOEL

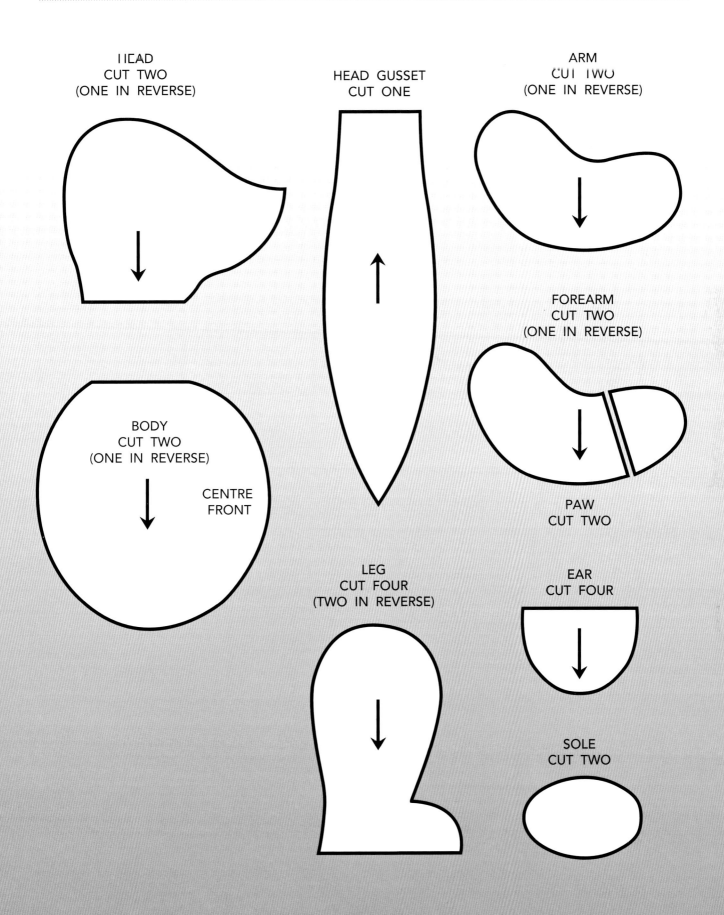

HEAD
CUT TWO
(ONE IN REVERSE)

HEAD GUSSET
CUT ONE

ARM
CUT TWO
(ONE IN REVERSE)

BODY
CUT TWO
(ONE IN REVERSE)

CENTRE
FRONT

FOREARM
CUT TWO
(ONE IN REVERSE)

PAW
CUT TWO

LEG
CUT FOUR
(TWO IN REVERSE)

EAR
CUT FOUR

SOLE
CUT TWO

JOSEPH

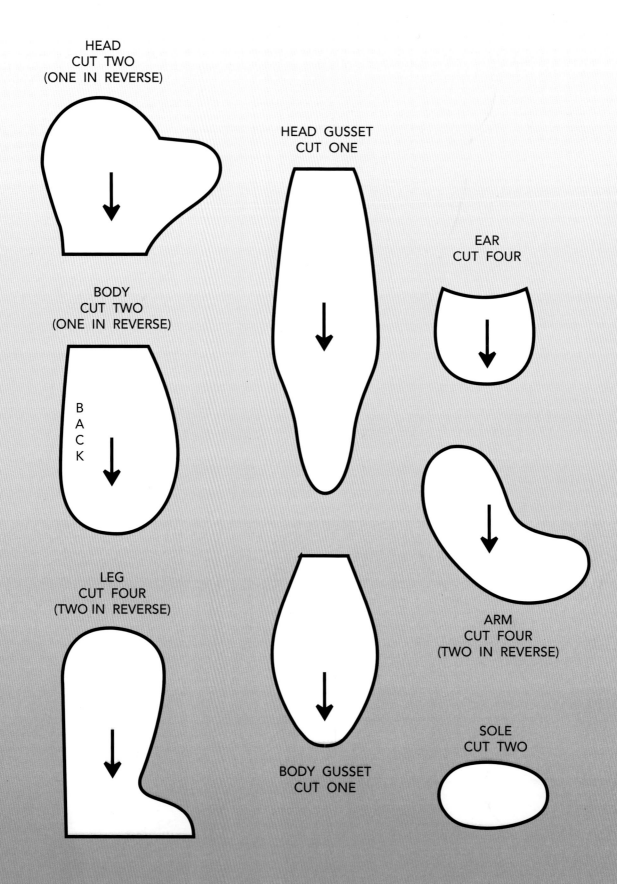

HEAD
CUT TWO
(ONE IN REVERSE)

HEAD GUSSET
CUT ONE

EAR
CUT FOUR

BODY
CUT TWO
(ONE IN REVERSE)

B
A
C
K

LEG
CUT FOUR
(TWO IN REVERSE)

ARM
CUT FOUR
(TWO IN REVERSE)

BODY GUSSET
CUT ONE

SOLE
CUT TWO

VALENTINE

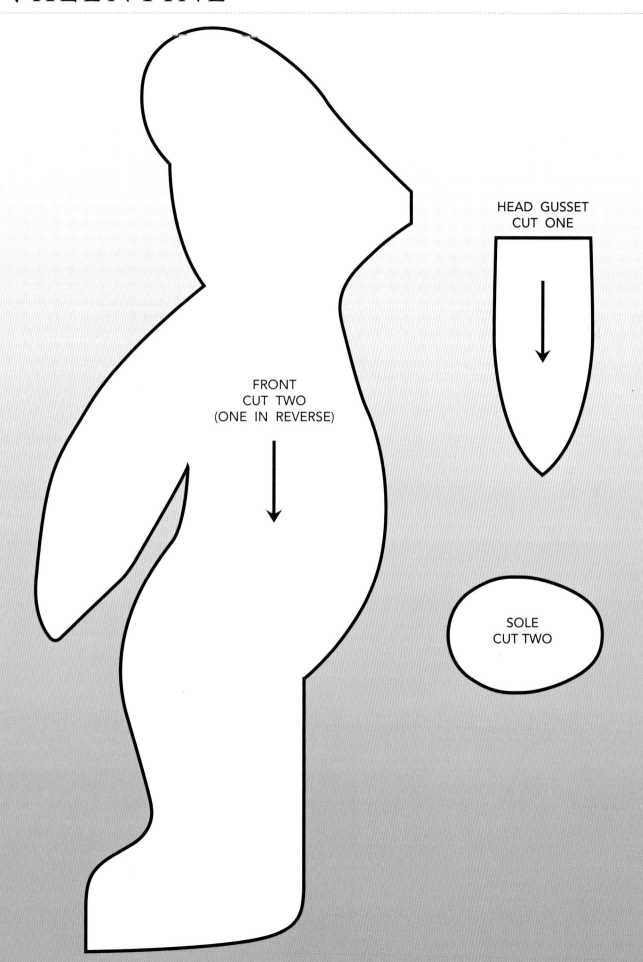

HEAD GUSSET
CUT ONE

FRONT
CUT TWO
(ONE IN REVERSE)

SOLE
CUT TWO

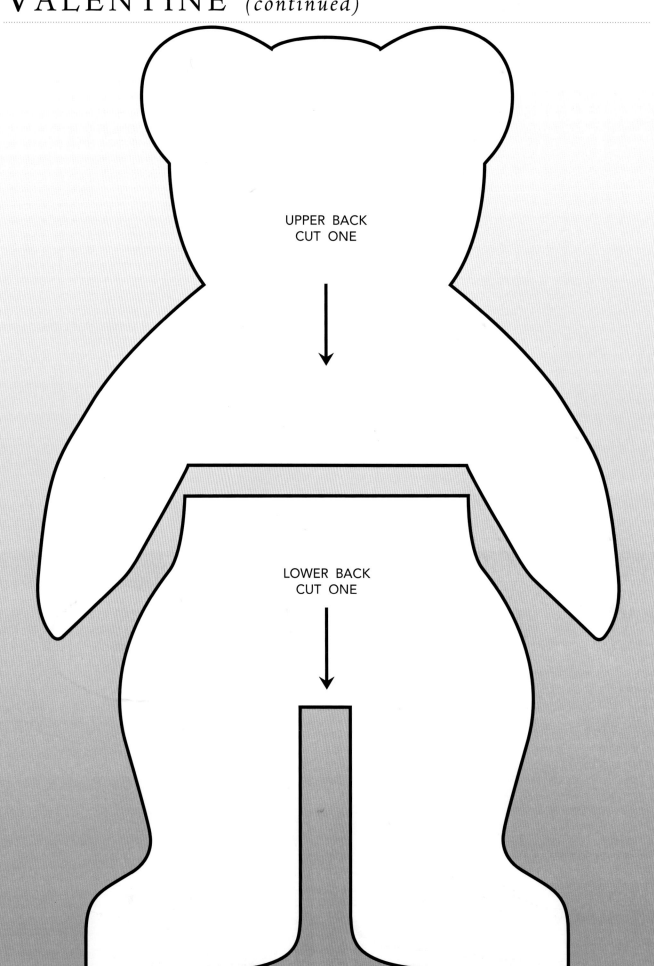

UPPER BACK
CUT ONE

LOWER BACK
CUT ONE

OLIVER

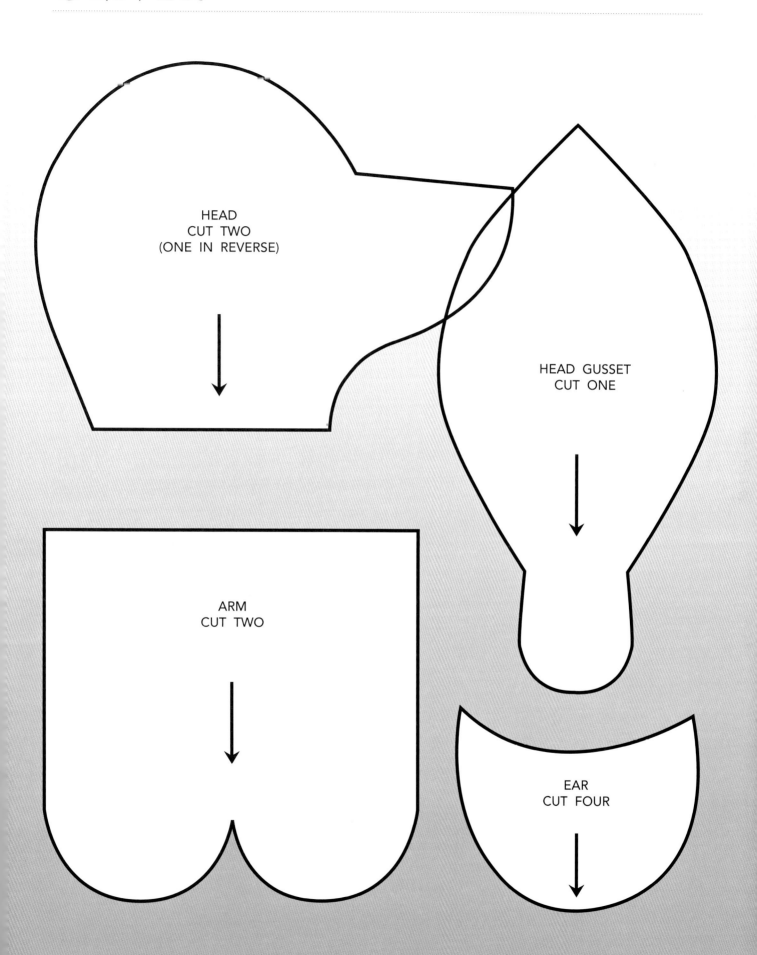

HEAD
CUT TWO
(ONE IN REVERSE)

HEAD GUSSET
CUT ONE

ARM
CUT TWO

EAR
CUT FOUR

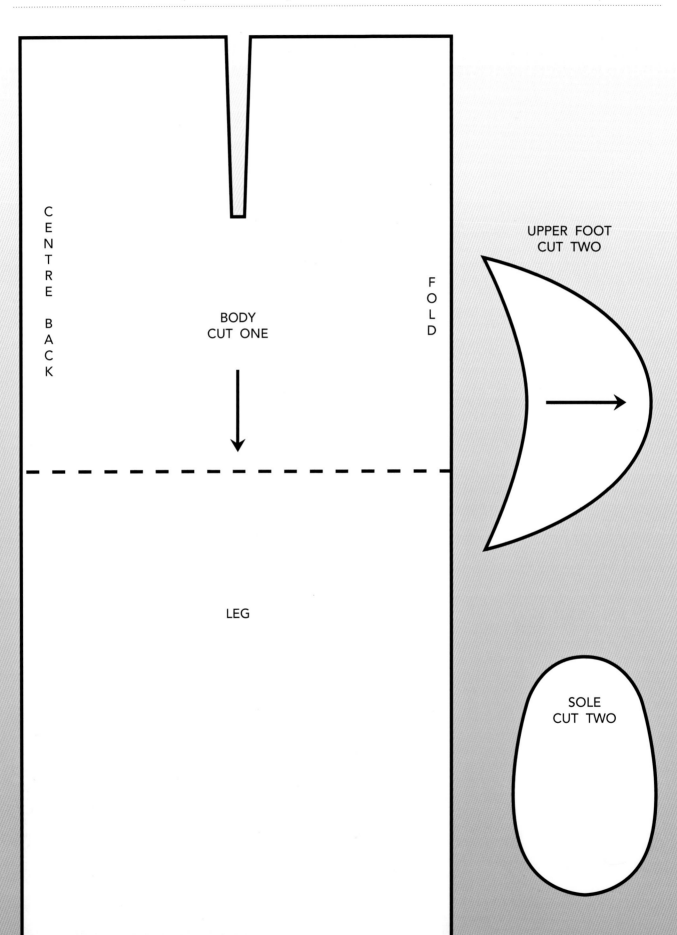

CENTRE BACK

FOLD

BODY
CUT ONE

LEG

UPPER FOOT
CUT TWO

SOLE
CUT TWO

PAUL

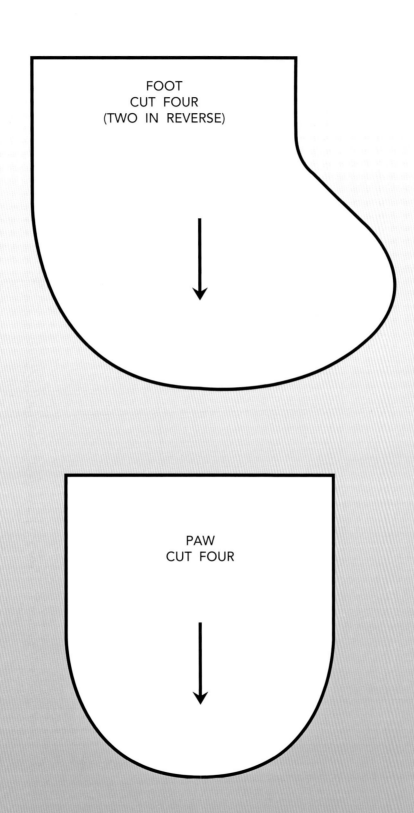

FOOT
CUT FOUR
(TWO IN REVERSE)

PAW
CUT FOUR

BRUMAS

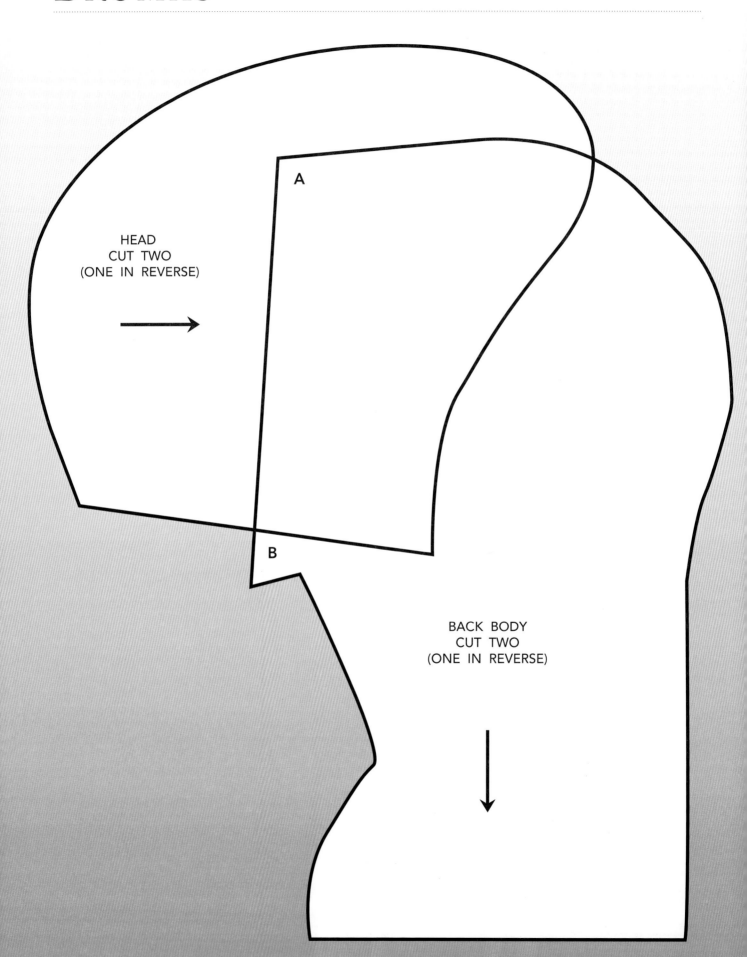

HEAD
CUT TWO
(ONE IN REVERSE)

A

B

BACK BODY
CUT TWO
(ONE IN REVERSE)

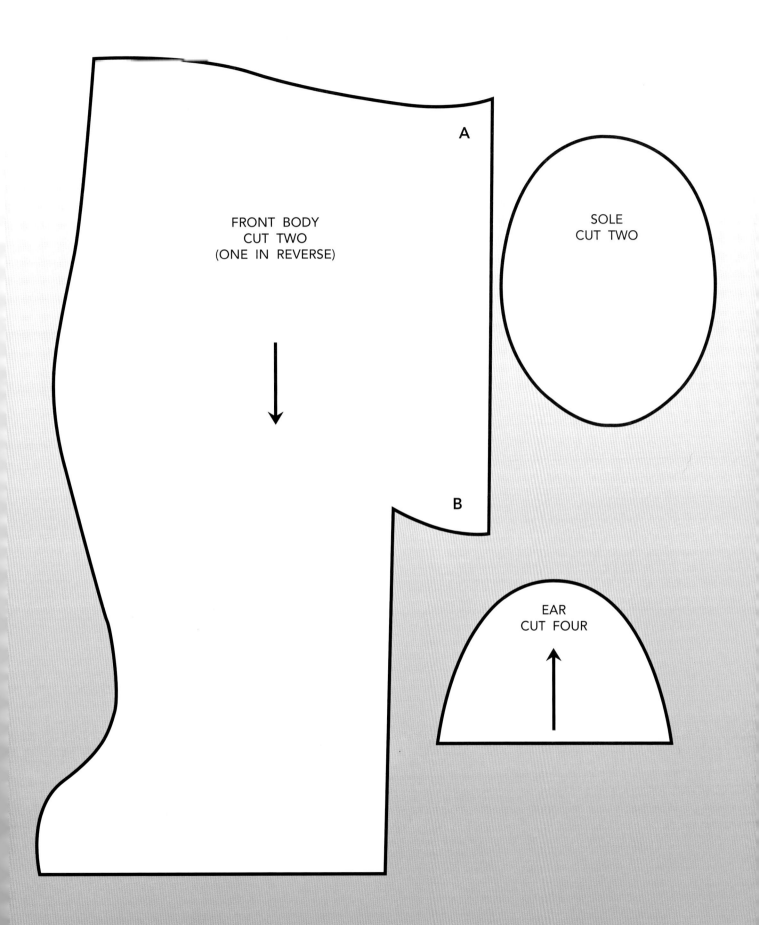

FRONT BODY
CUT TWO
(ONE IN REVERSE)

A

B

SOLE
CUT TWO

EAR
CUT FOUR

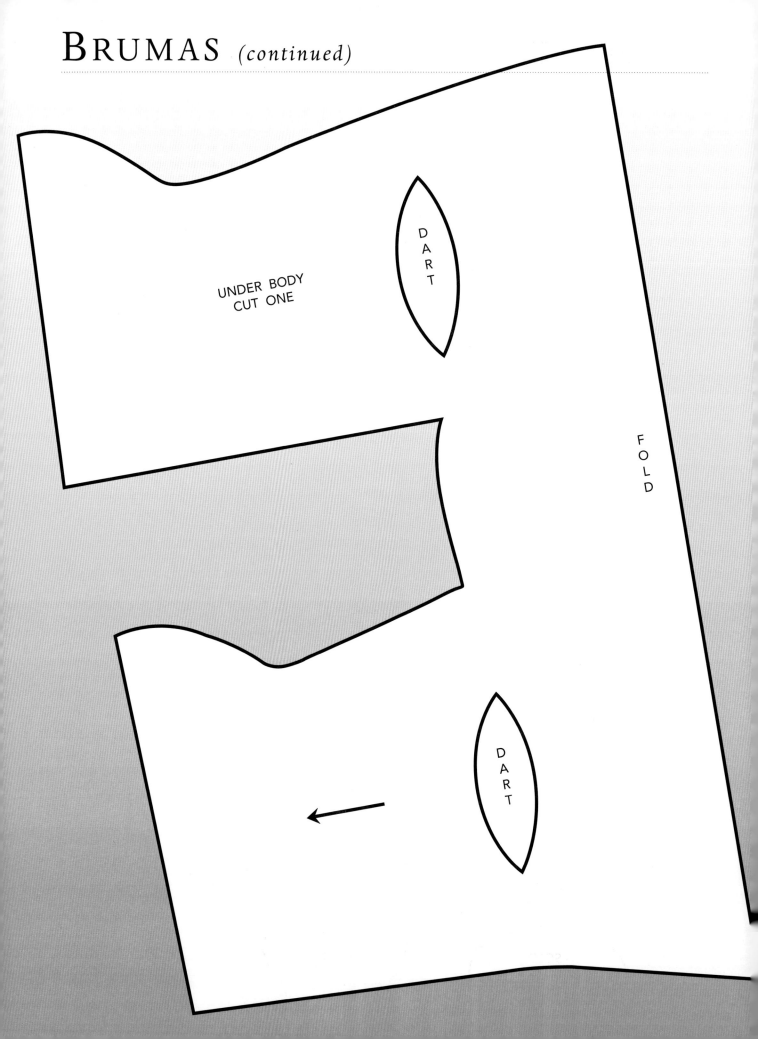

DART

UNDER BODY
CUT ONE

FOLD

DART

GEORGIE

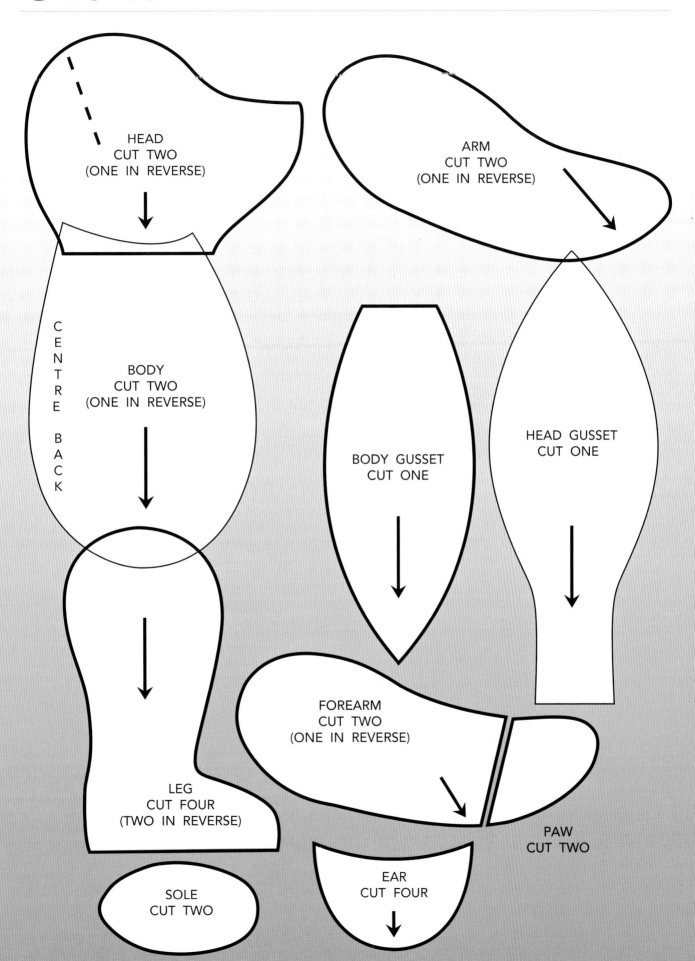

HEAD
CUT TWO
(ONE IN REVERSE)

ARM
CUT TWO
(ONE IN REVERSE)

C E N T R E   B A C K

BODY
CUT TWO
(ONE IN REVERSE)

BODY GUSSET
CUT ONE

HEAD GUSSET
CUT ONE

FOREARM
CUT TWO
(ONE IN REVERSE)

PAW
CUT TWO

LEG
CUT FOUR
(TWO IN REVERSE)

SOLE
CUT TWO

EAR
CUT FOUR

BERTIE

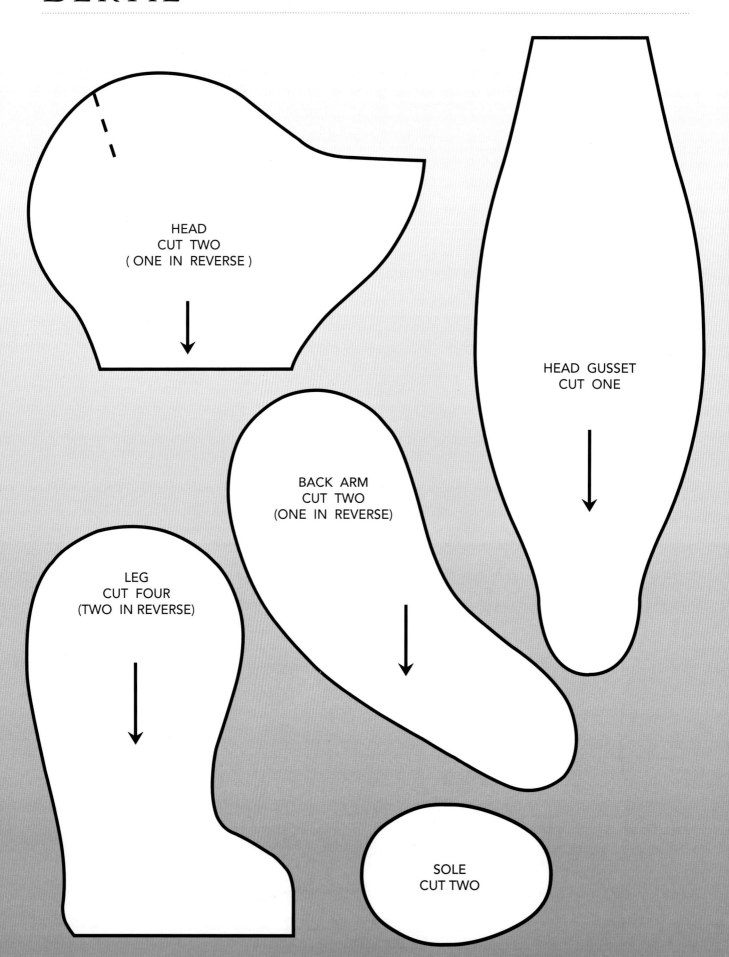

HEAD
CUT TWO
(ONE IN REVERSE)

HEAD GUSSET
CUT ONE

BACK ARM
CUT TWO
(ONE IN REVERSE)

LEG
CUT FOUR
(TWO IN REVERSE)

SOLE
CUT TWO

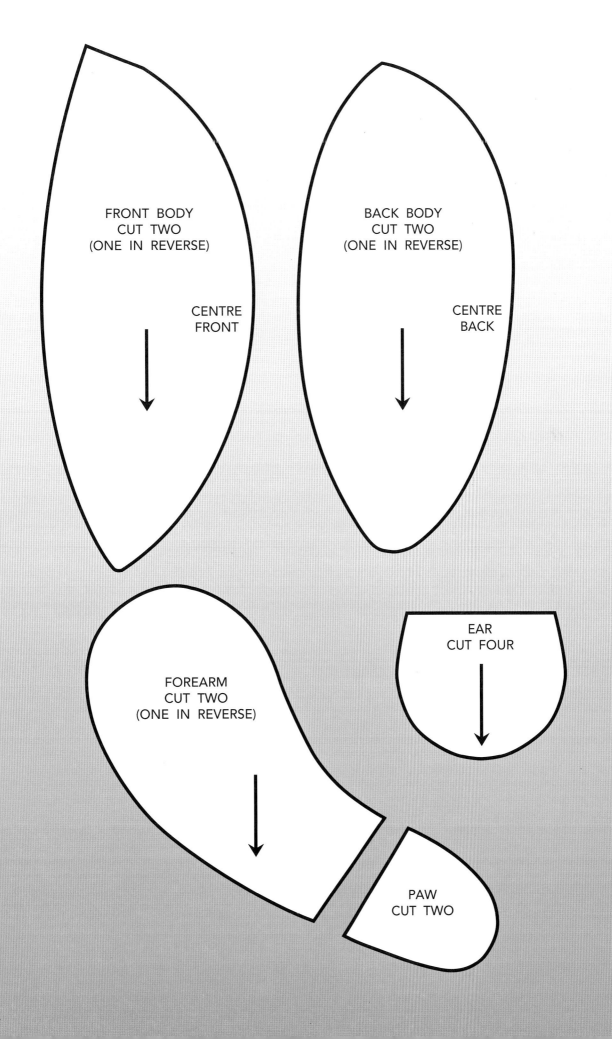

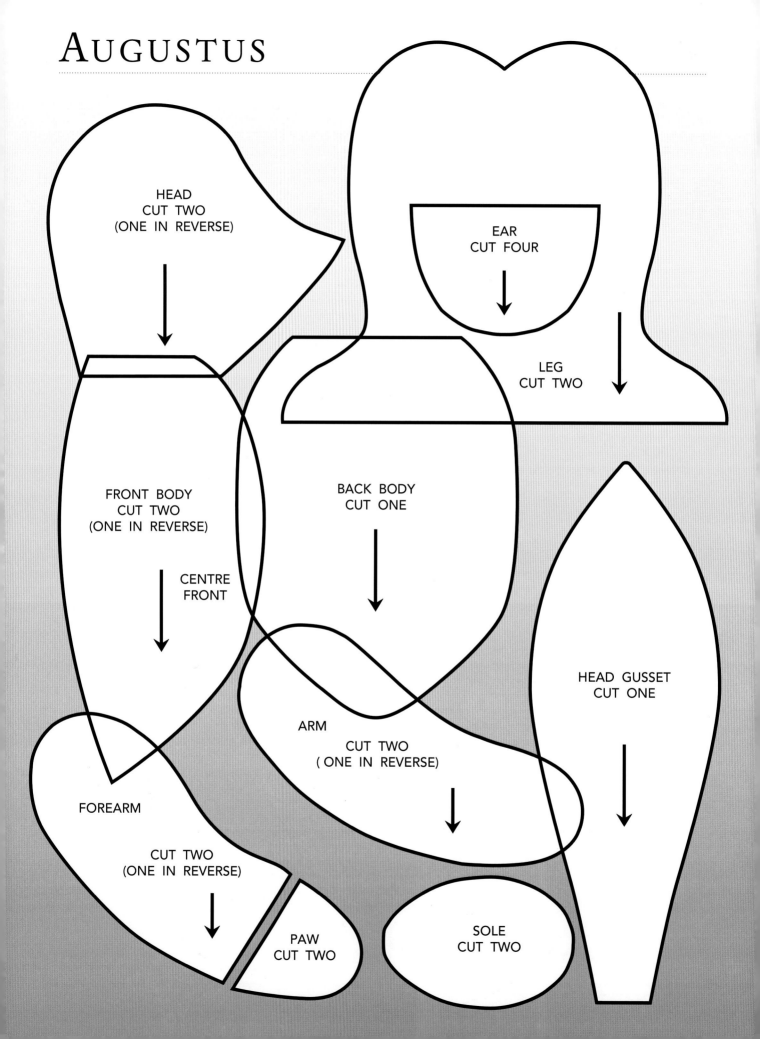

WILLIAM

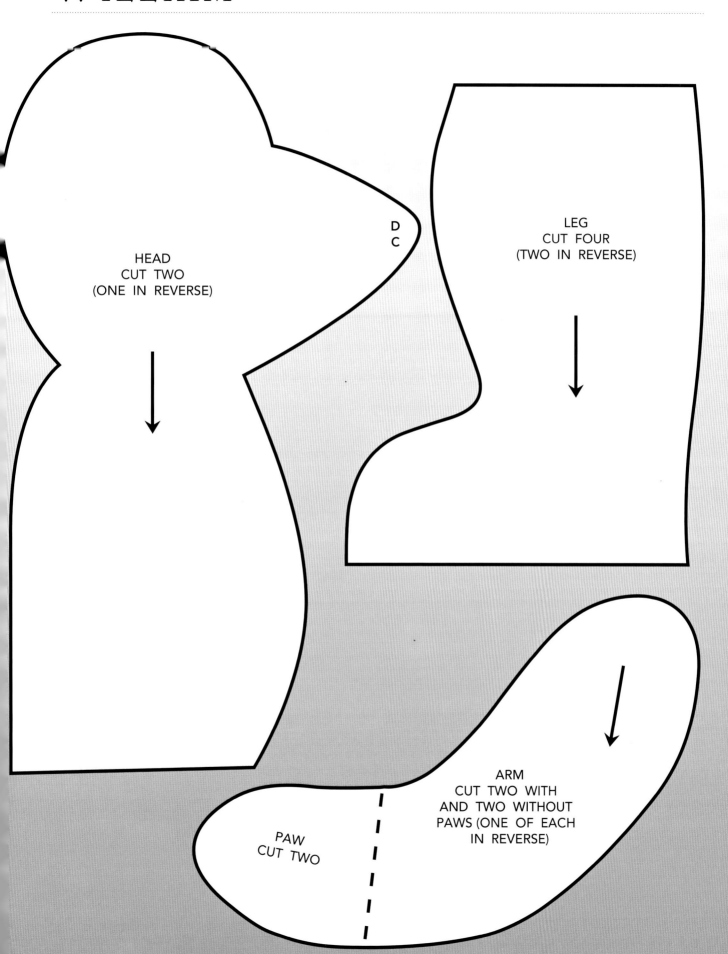

HEAD
CUT TWO
(ONE IN REVERSE)

D
C

LEG
CUT FOUR
(TWO IN REVERSE)

PAW
CUT TWO

ARM
CUT TWO WITH
AND TWO WITHOUT
PAWS (ONE OF EACH
IN REVERSE)

WILLIAM *(continued)*

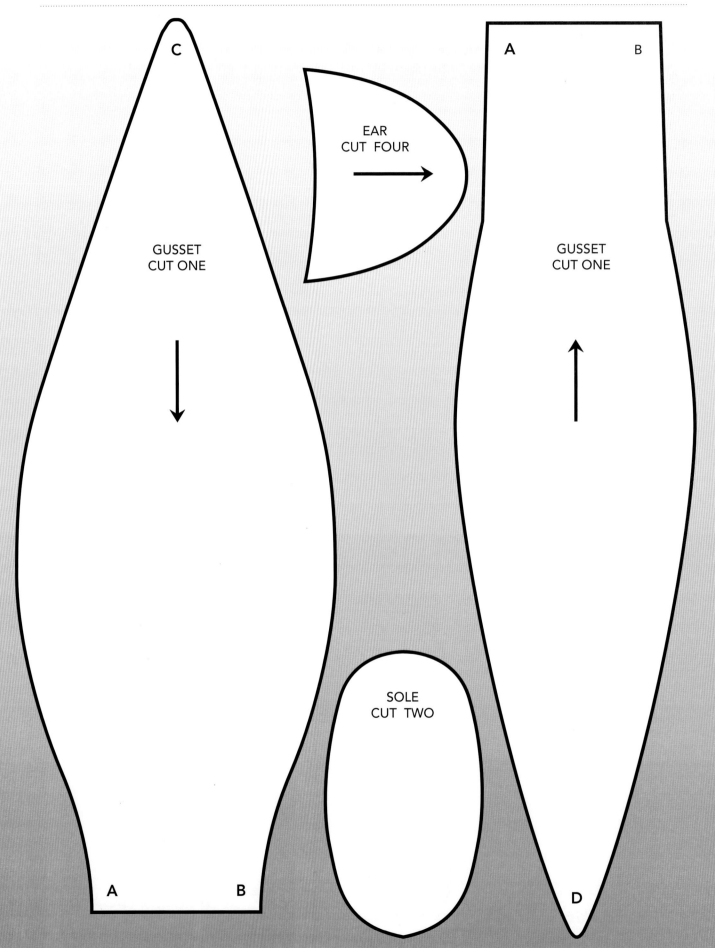

C

EAR
CUT FOUR

A   B

GUSSET
CUT ONE

GUSSET
CUT ONE

SOLE
CUT TWO

A   B

D

TIMOTHY

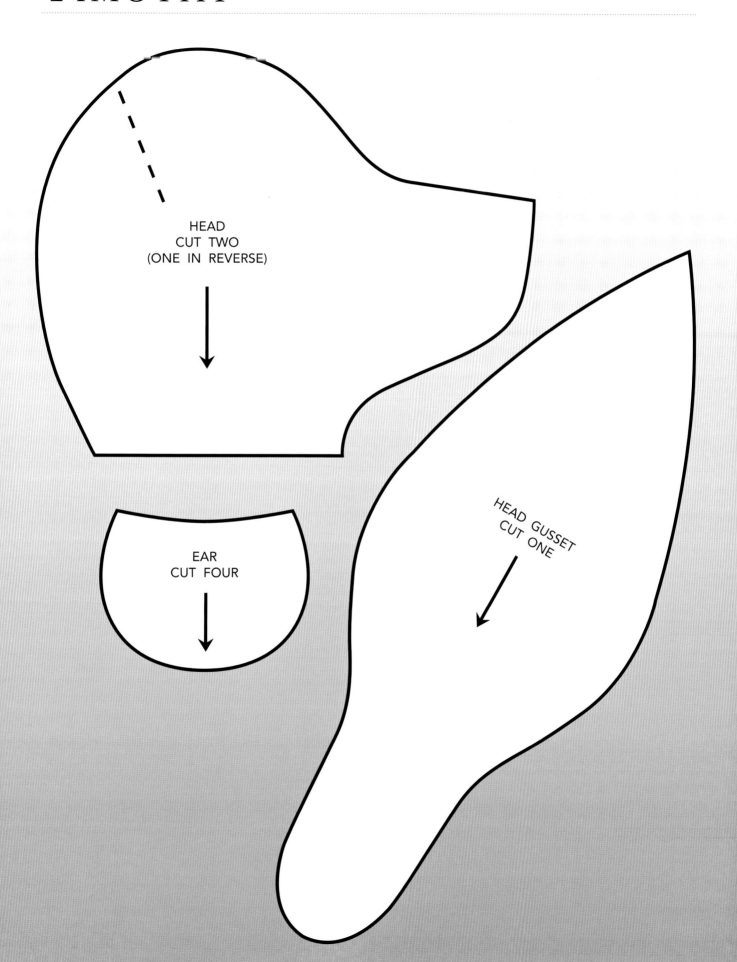

HEAD
CUT TWO
(ONE IN REVERSE)

EAR
CUT FOUR

HEAD GUSSET
CUT ONE

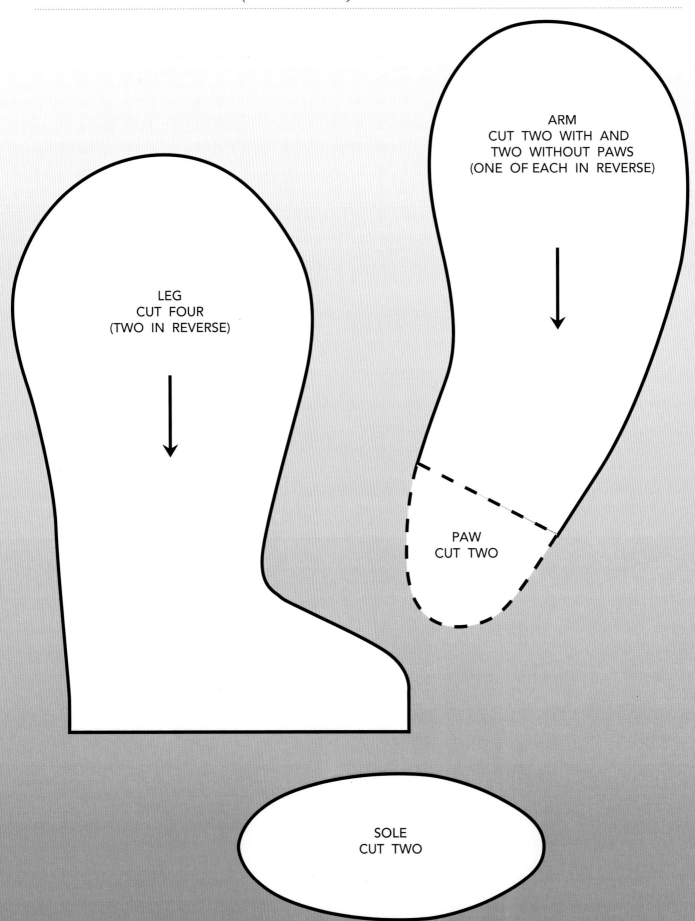

ARM
CUT TWO WITH AND
TWO WITHOUT PAWS
(ONE OF EACH IN REVERSE)

LEG
CUT FOUR
(TWO IN REVERSE)

PAW
CUT TWO

SOLE
CUT TWO

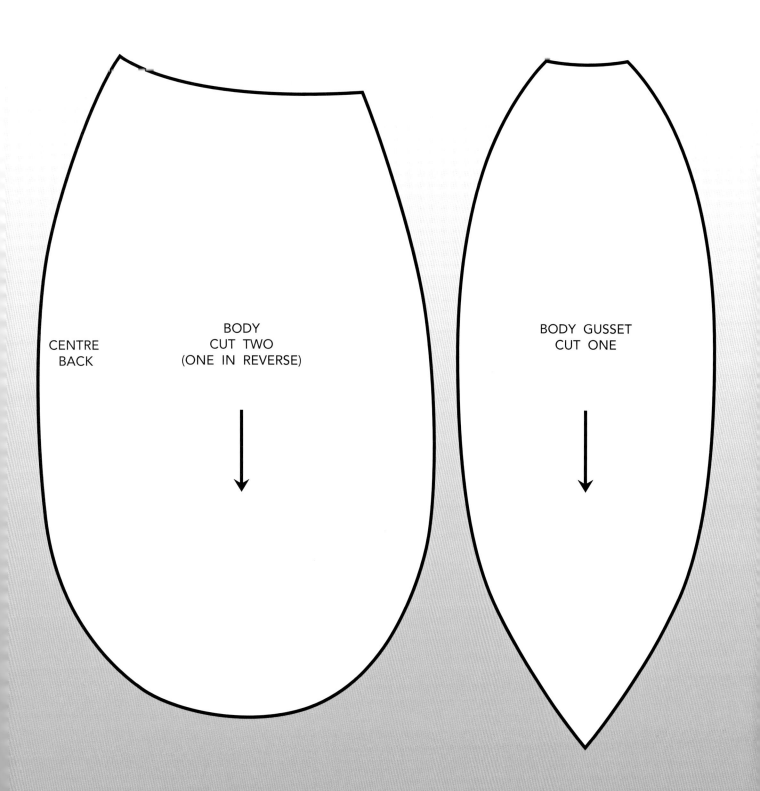

CENTRE
BACK

BODY
CUT TWO
(ONE IN REVERSE)

BODY GUSSET
CUT ONE

ALBERT

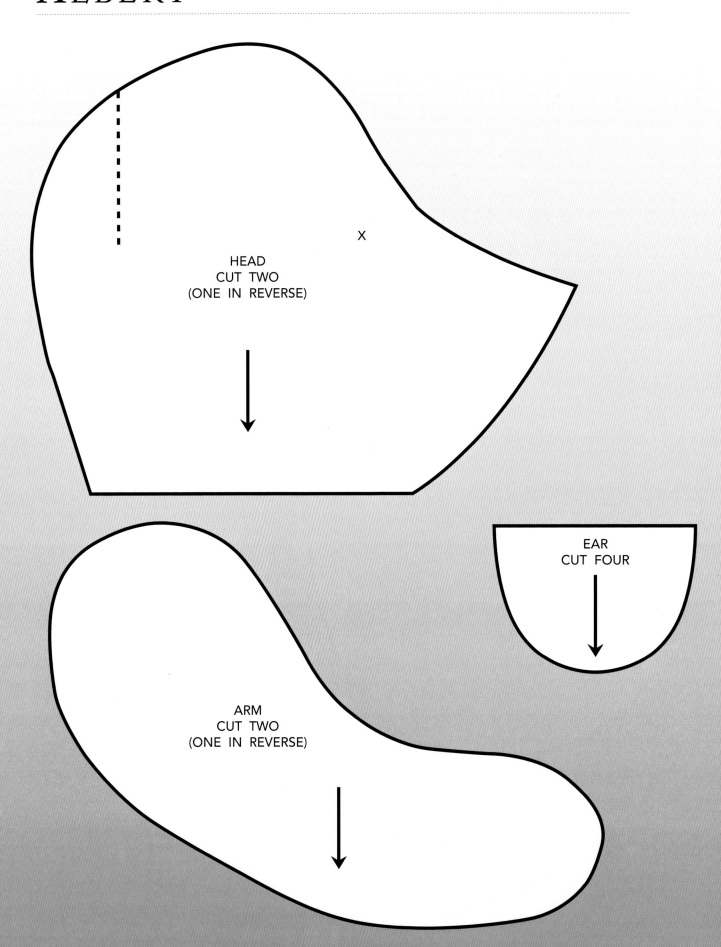

HEAD
CUT TWO
(ONE IN REVERSE)

X

EAR
CUT FOUR

ARM
CUT TWO
(ONE IN REVERSE)

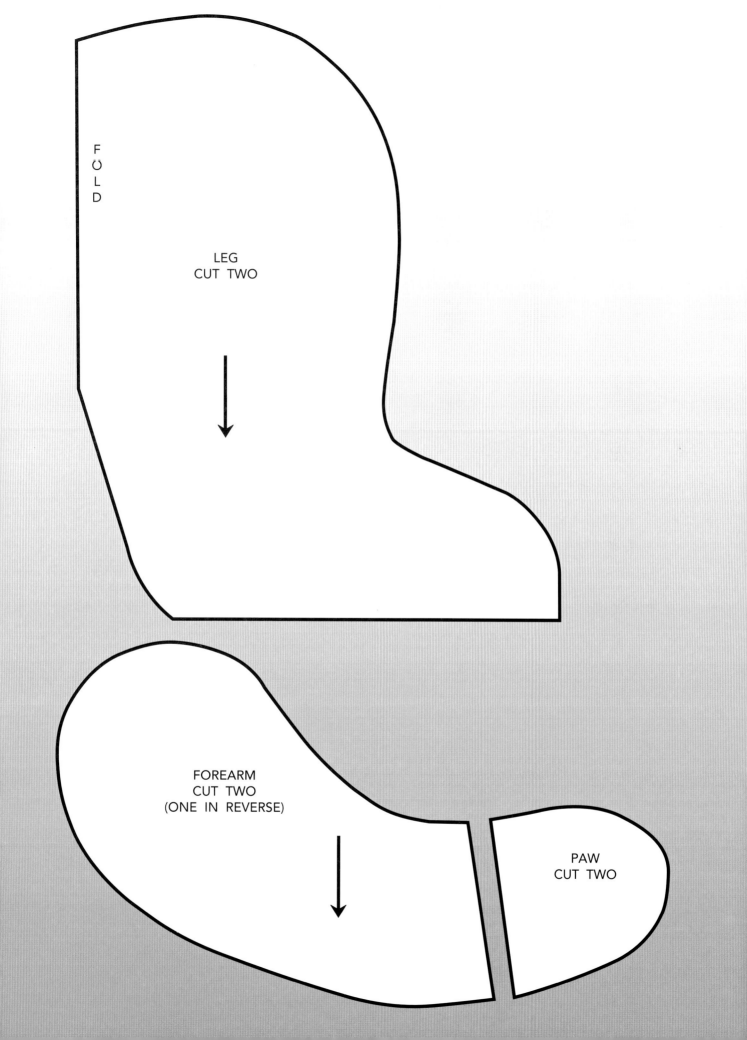

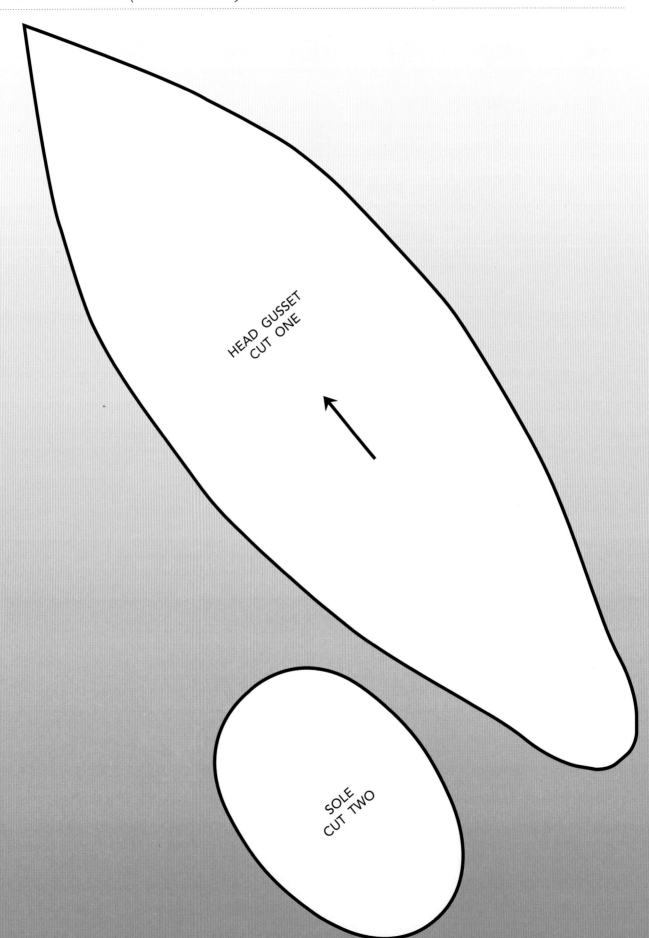

HEAD GUSSET
CUT ONE

SOLE
CUT TWO

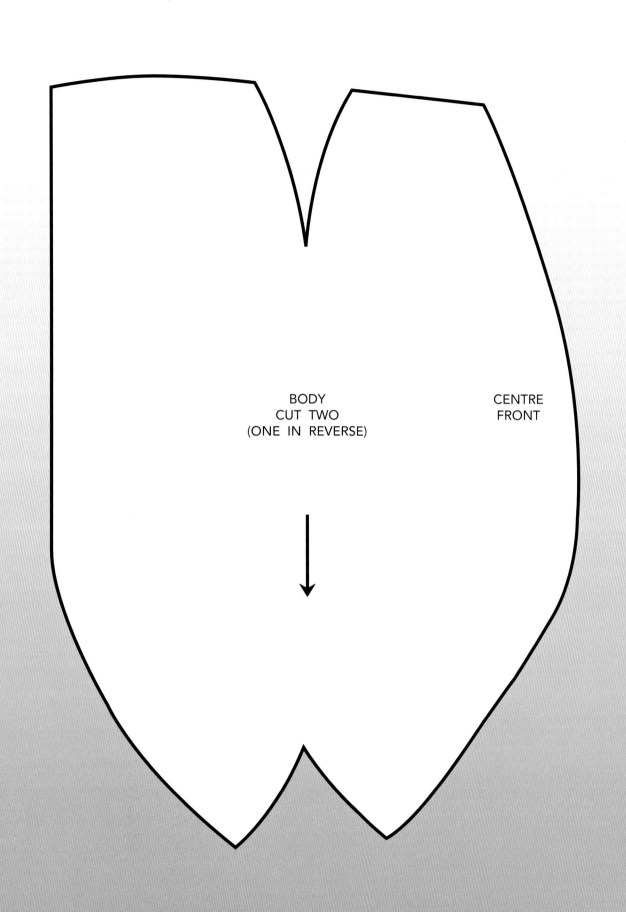

BODY
CUT TWO
(ONE IN REVERSE)

CENTRE
FRONT

HENRY

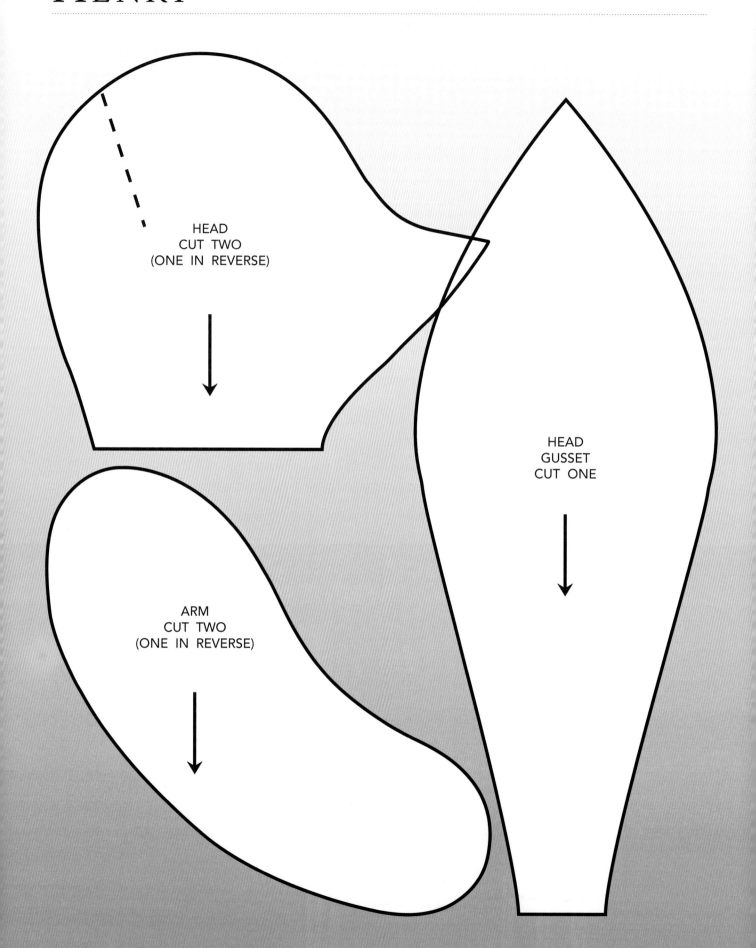

HEAD
CUT TWO
(ONE IN REVERSE)

HEAD
GUSSET
CUT ONE

ARM
CUT TWO
(ONE IN REVERSE)

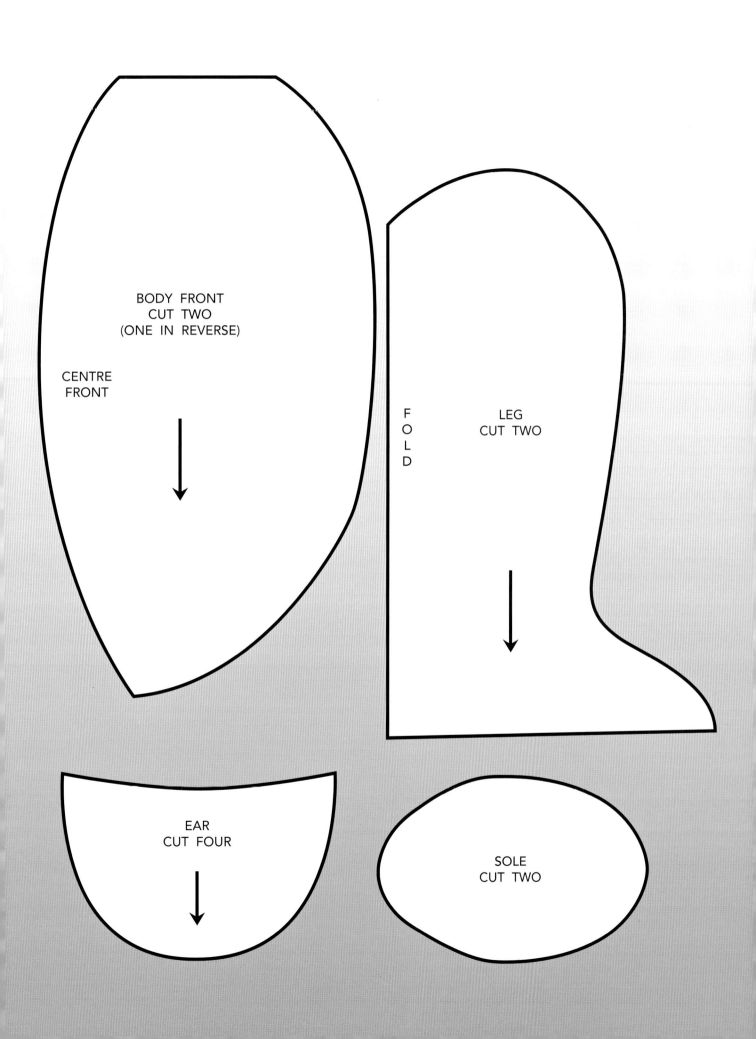

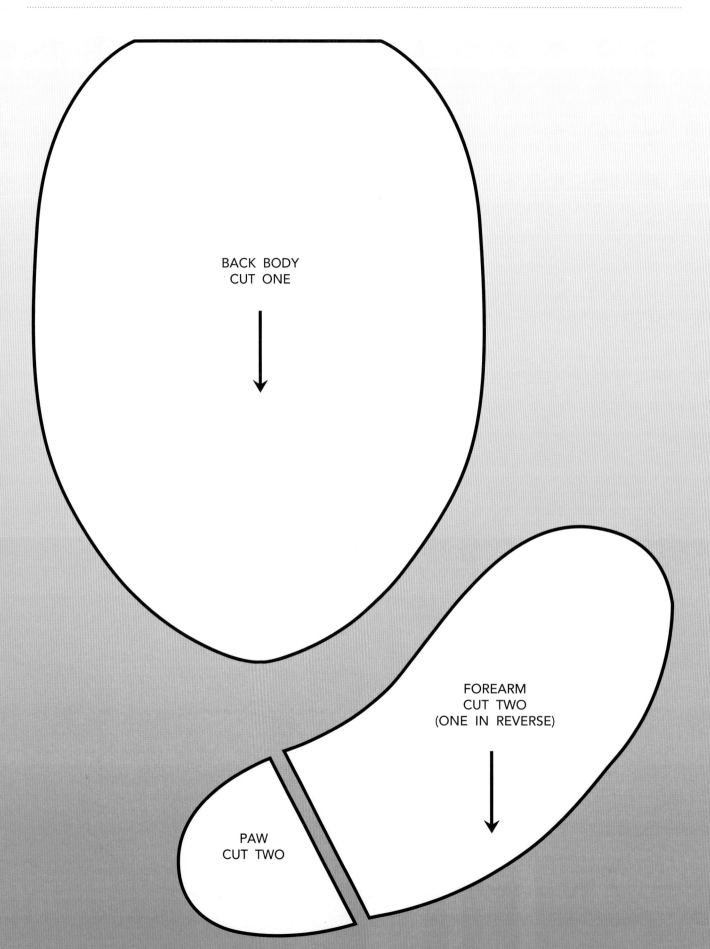

BACK BODY
CUT ONE

FOREARM
CUT TWO
(ONE IN REVERSE)

PAW
CUT TWO

Marmaduke

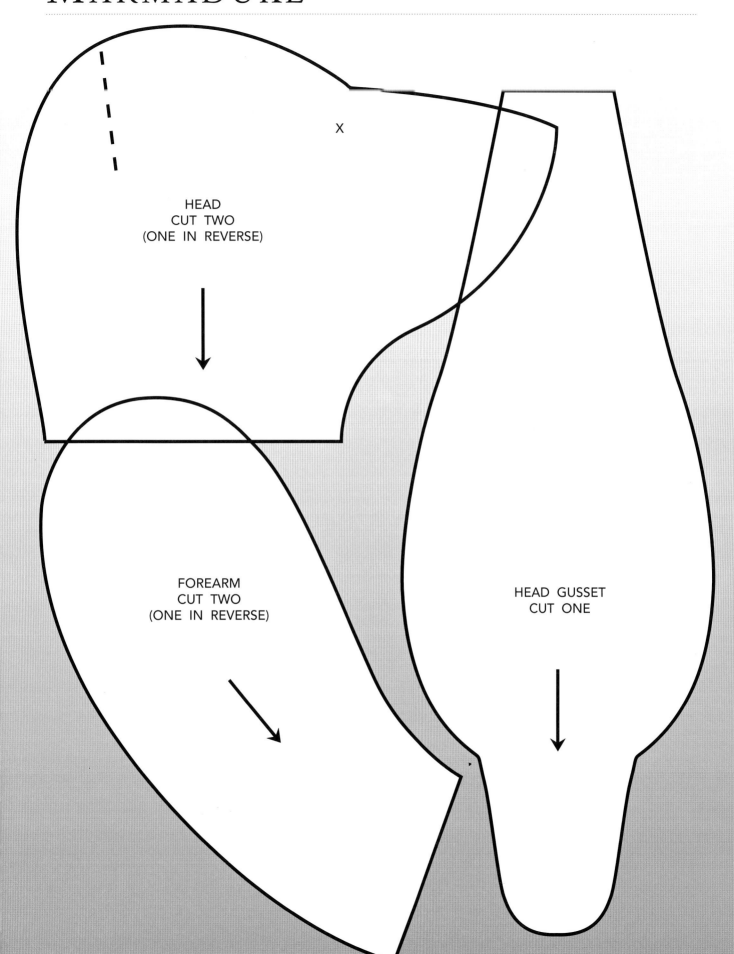

X

HEAD
CUT TWO
(ONE IN REVERSE)

FOREARM
CUT TWO
(ONE IN REVERSE)

HEAD GUSSET
CUT ONE

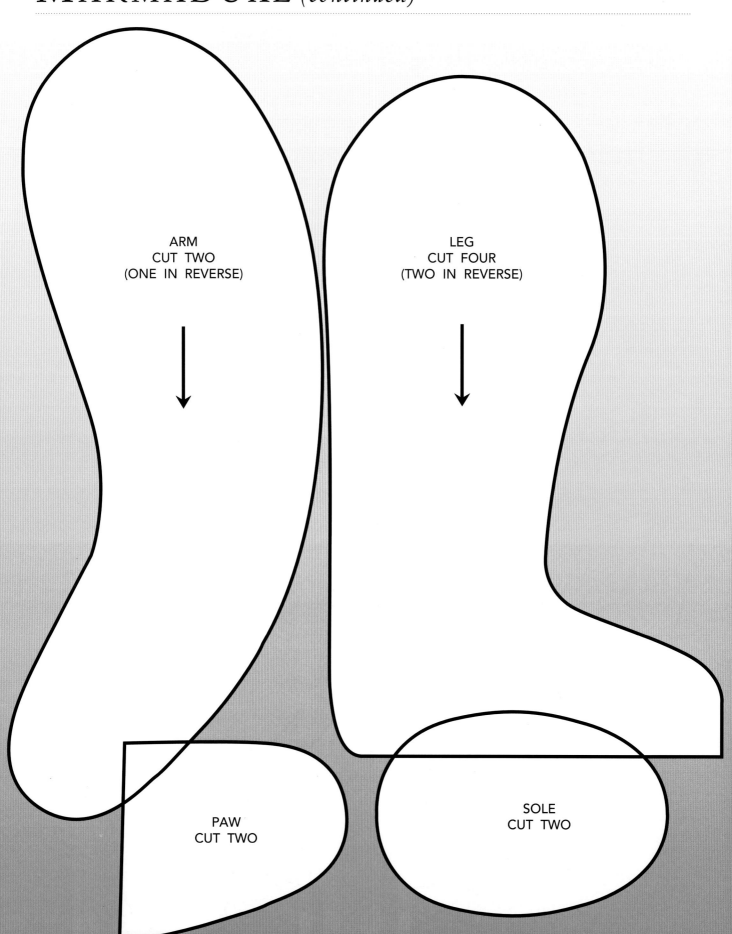

ARM
CUT TWO
(ONE IN REVERSE)

LEG
CUT FOUR
(TWO IN REVERSE)

PAW
CUT TWO

SOLE
CUT TWO

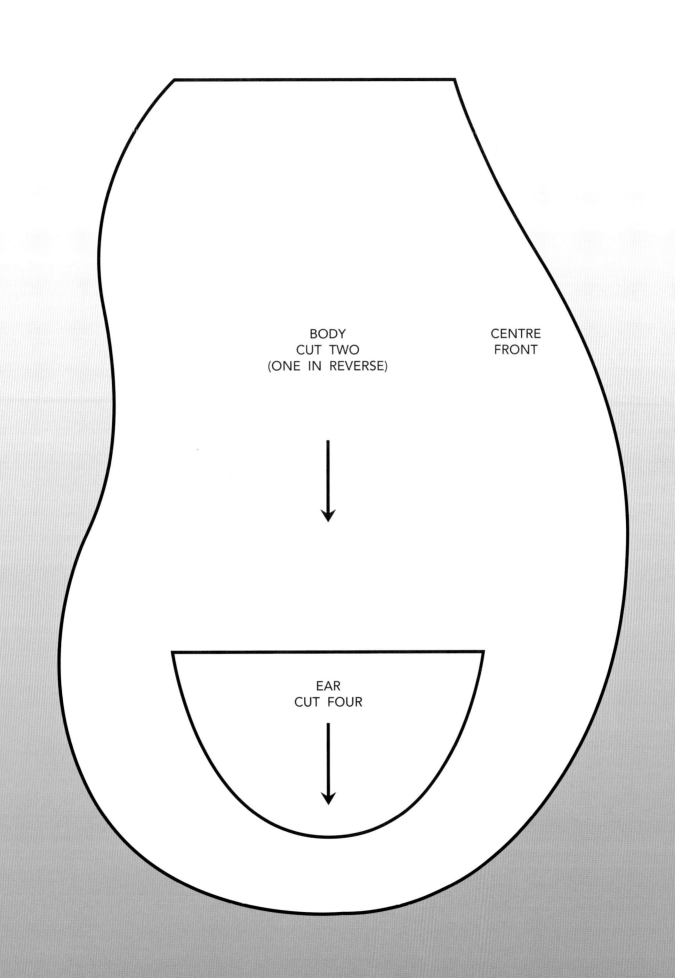

BODY
CUT TWO
(ONE IN REVERSE)

CENTRE
FRONT

EAR
CUT FOUR

EDWARD

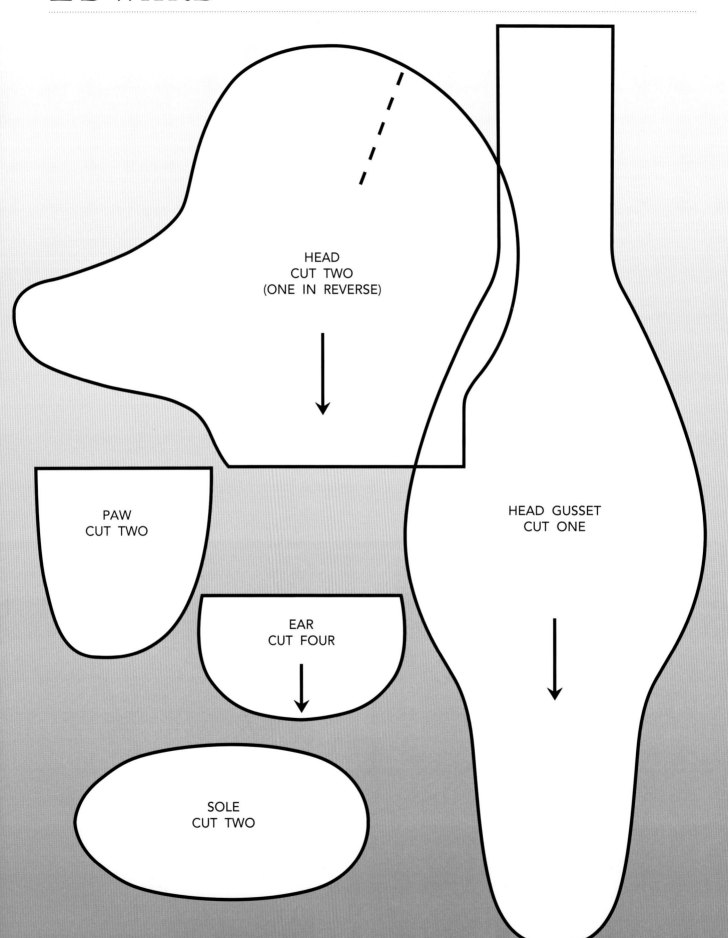

HEAD
CUT TWO
(ONE IN REVERSE)

HEAD GUSSET
CUT ONE

PAW
CUT TWO

EAR
CUT FOUR

SOLE
CUT TWO

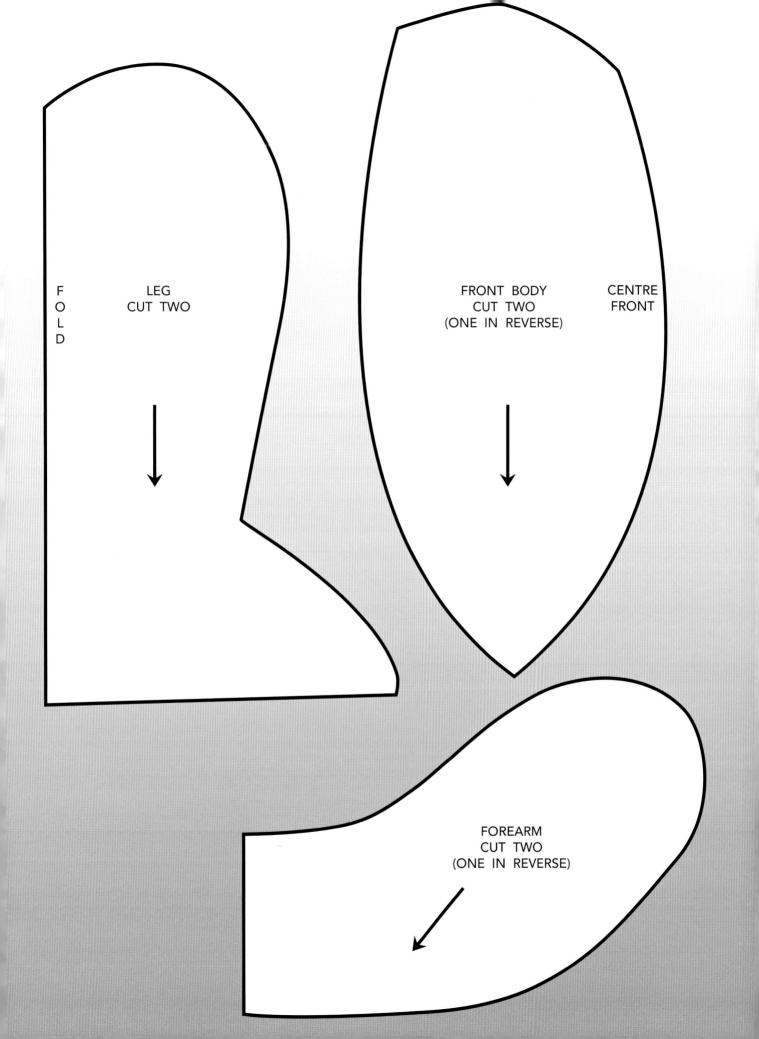

F
O
L
D

LEG
CUT TWO

FRONT BODY
CUT TWO
(ONE IN REVERSE)

CENTRE
FRONT

FOREARM
CUT TWO
(ONE IN REVERSE)

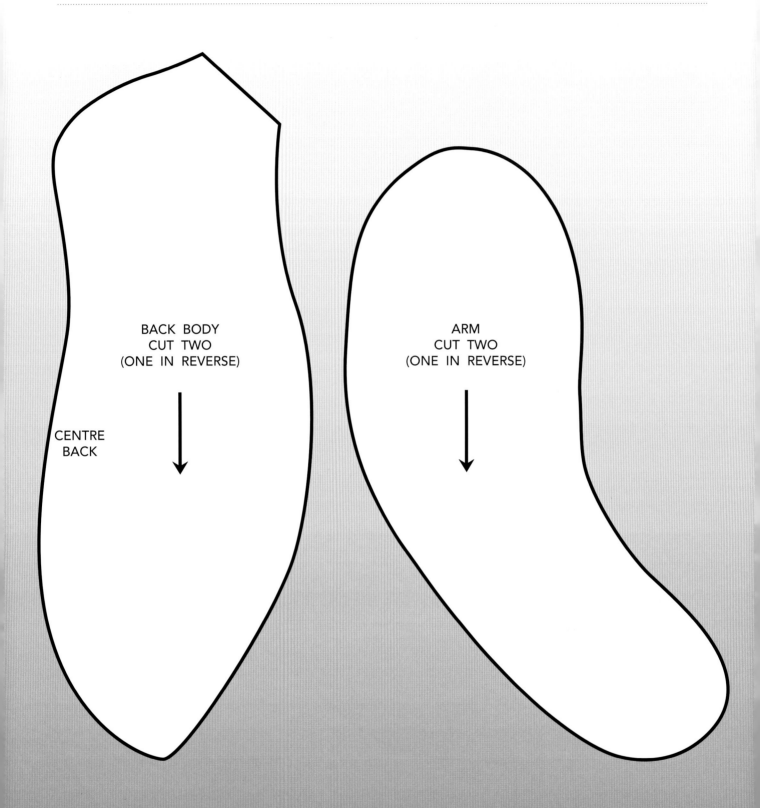

BACK BODY
CUT TWO
(ONE IN REVERSE)

CENTRE
BACK

ARM
CUT TWO
(ONE IN REVERSE)

RUBEN

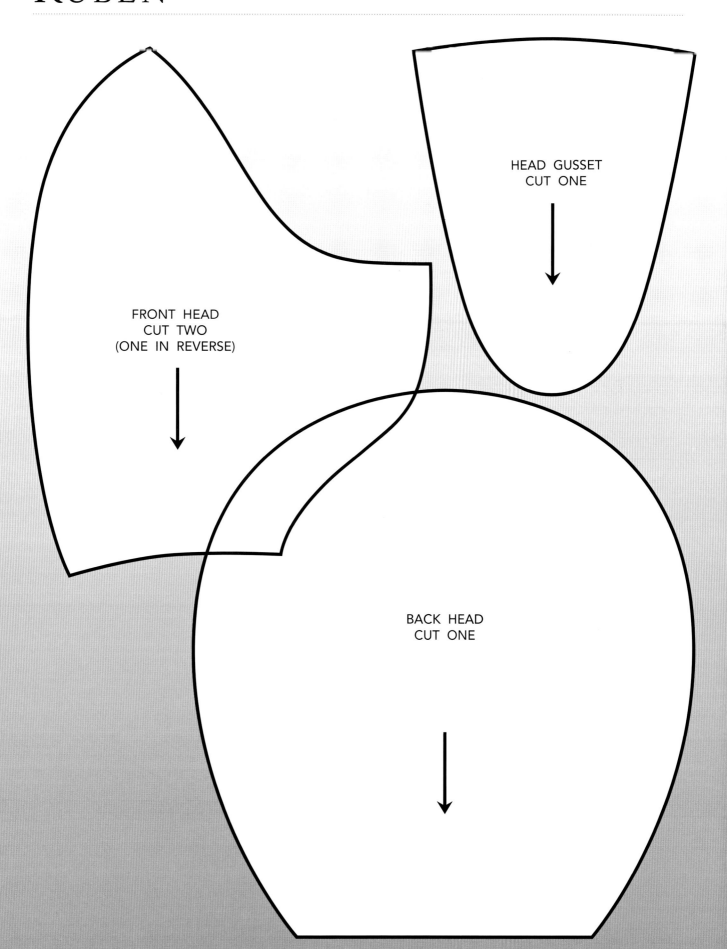

HEAD GUSSET
CUT ONE

FRONT HEAD
CUT TWO
(ONE IN REVERSE)

BACK HEAD
CUT ONE

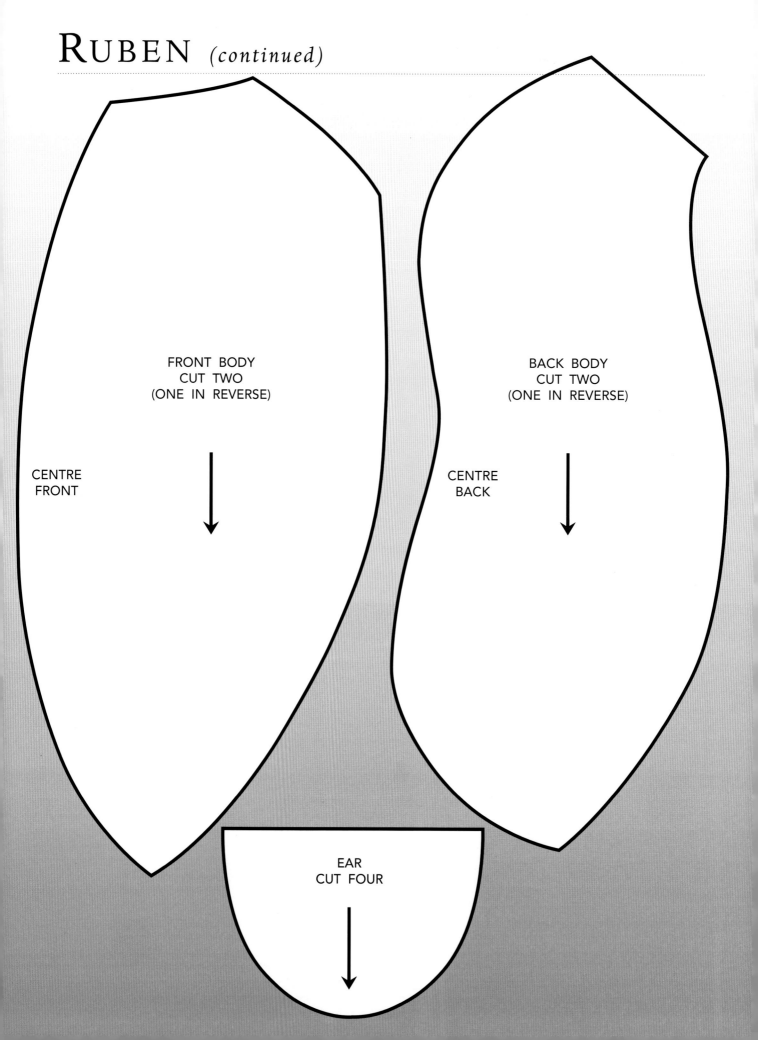

FRONT BODY
CUT TWO
(ONE IN REVERSE)

CENTRE
FRONT

BACK BODY
CUT TWO
(ONE IN REVERSE)

CENTRE
BACK

EAR
CUT FOUR

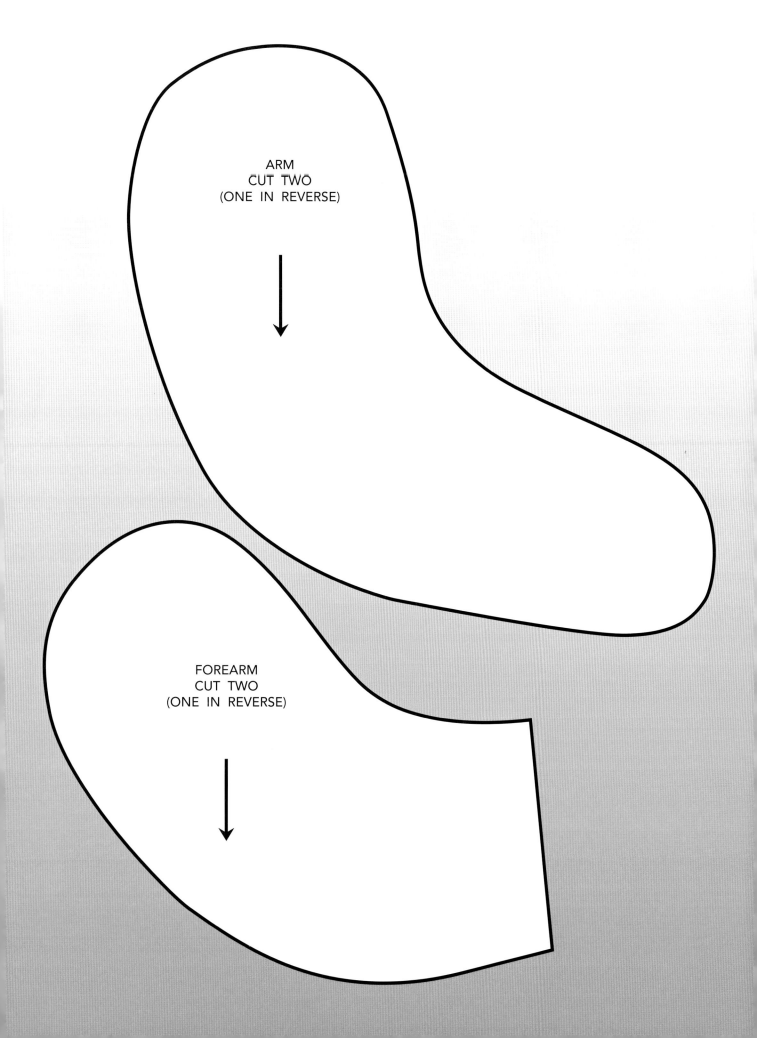

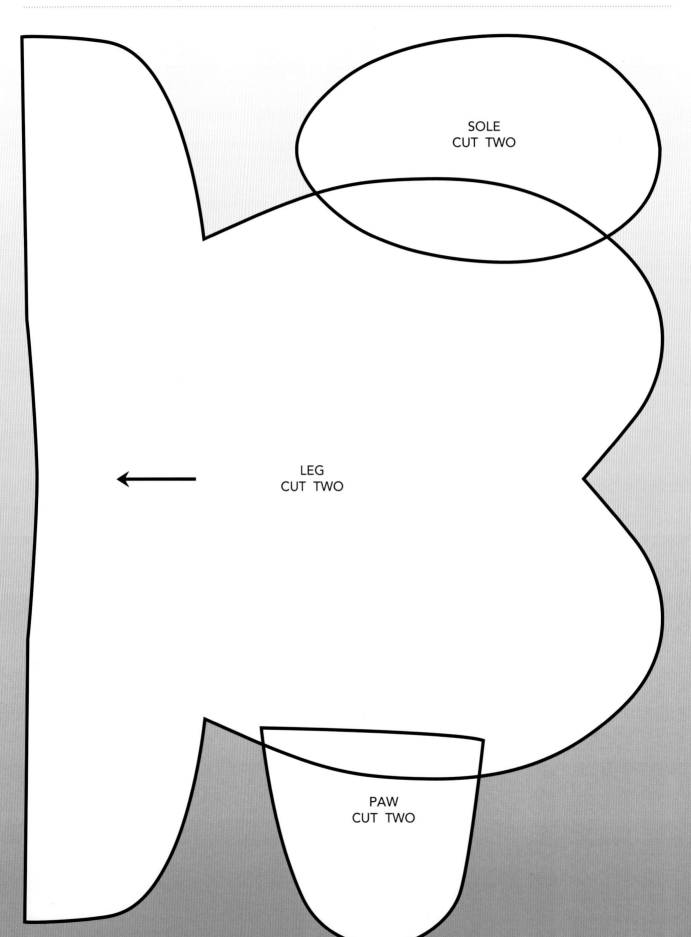

SOLE
CUT TWO

LEG
CUT TWO

PAW
CUT TWO

SEPTIMUS

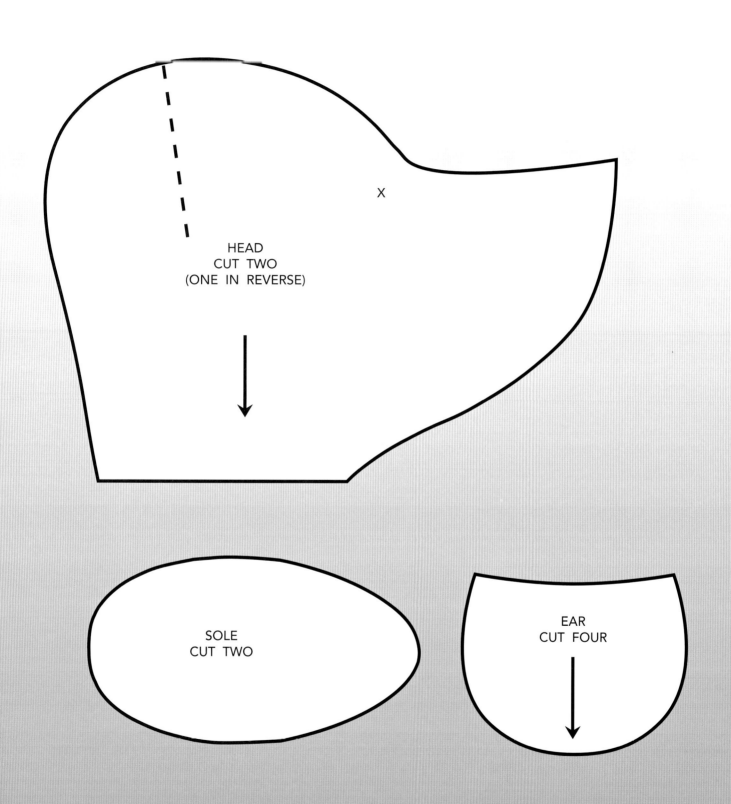

X

HEAD
CUT TWO
(ONE IN REVERSE)

SOLE
CUT TWO

EAR
CUT FOUR

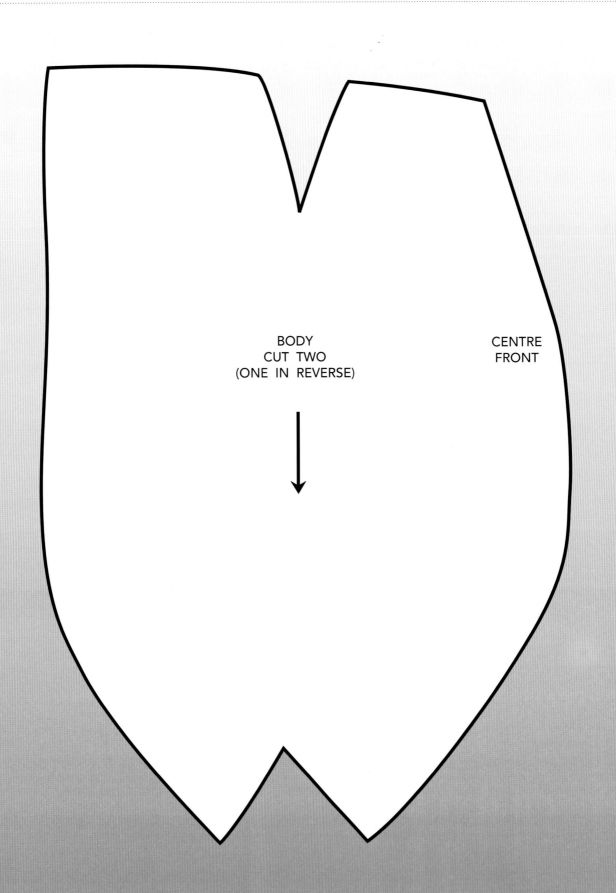

BODY
CUT TWO
(ONE IN REVERSE)

CENTRE
FRONT

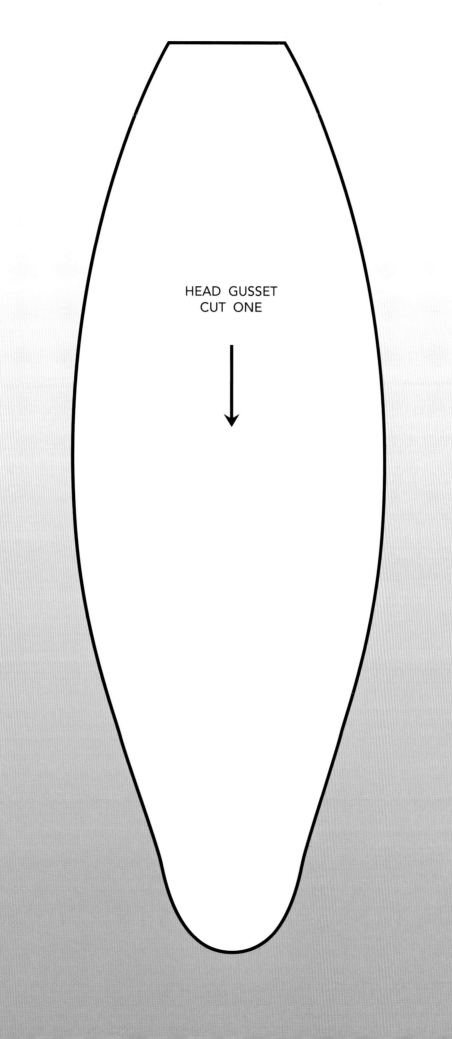

HEAD GUSSET
CUT ONE

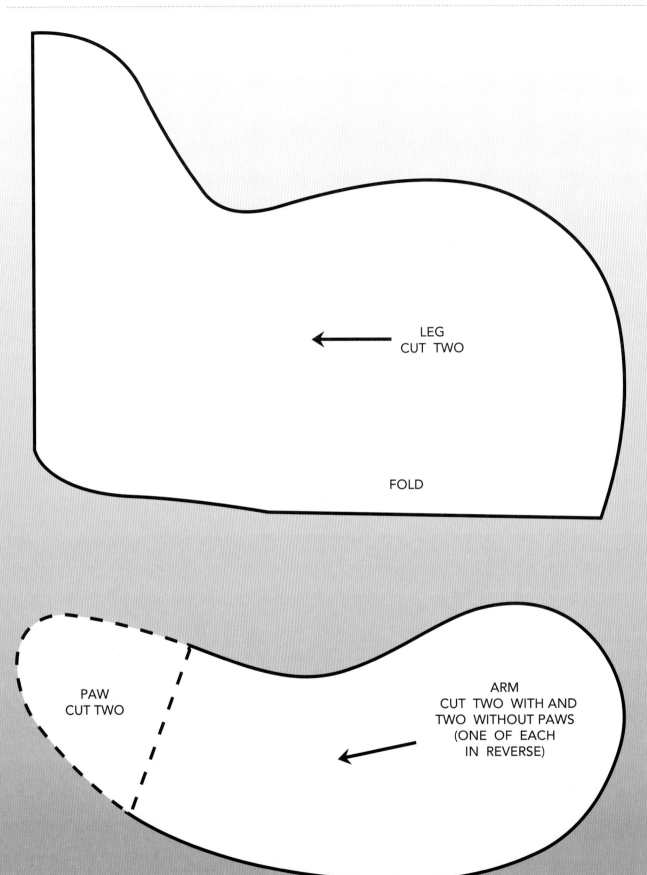

LEG
CUT TWO

FOLD

PAW
CUT TWO

ARM
CUT TWO WITH AND
TWO WITHOUT PAWS
(ONE OF EACH
IN REVERSE)

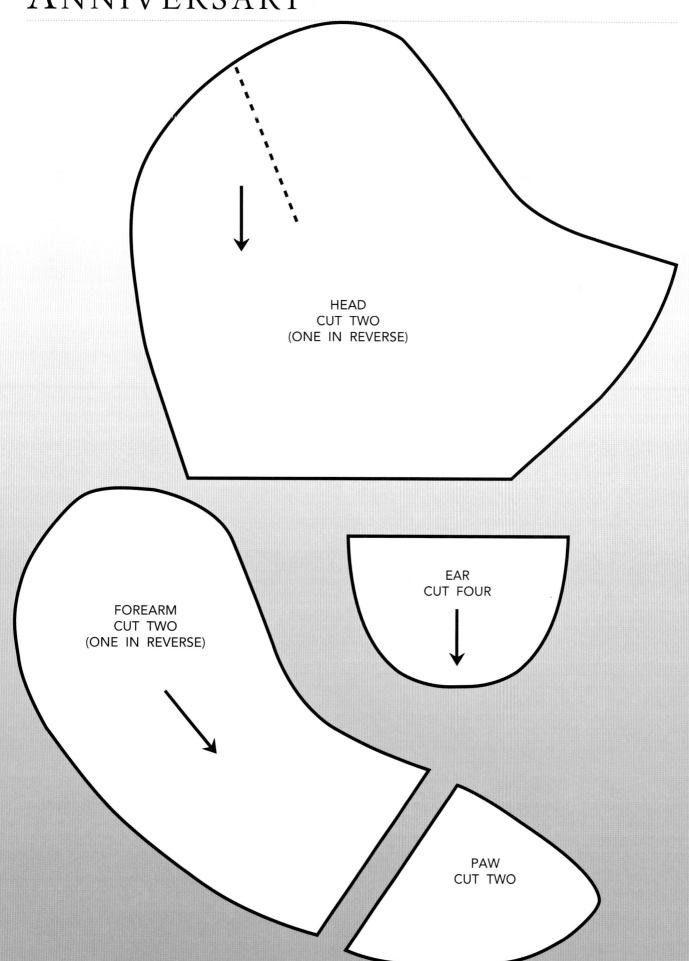

HEAD
CUT TWO
(ONE IN REVERSE)

FOREARM
CUT TWO
(ONE IN REVERSE)

EAR
CUT FOUR

PAW
CUT TWO

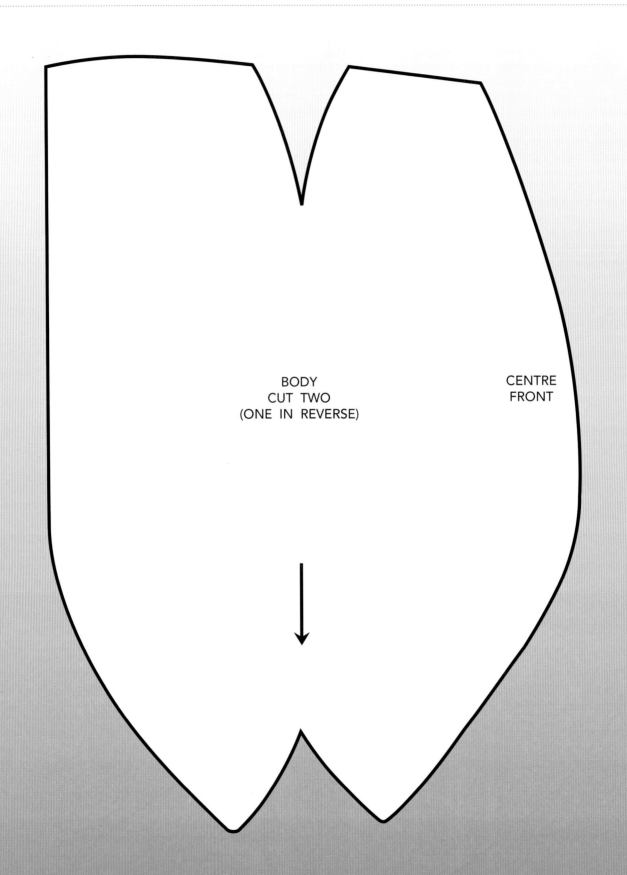

BODY
CUT TWO
(ONE IN REVERSE)

CENTRE
FRONT

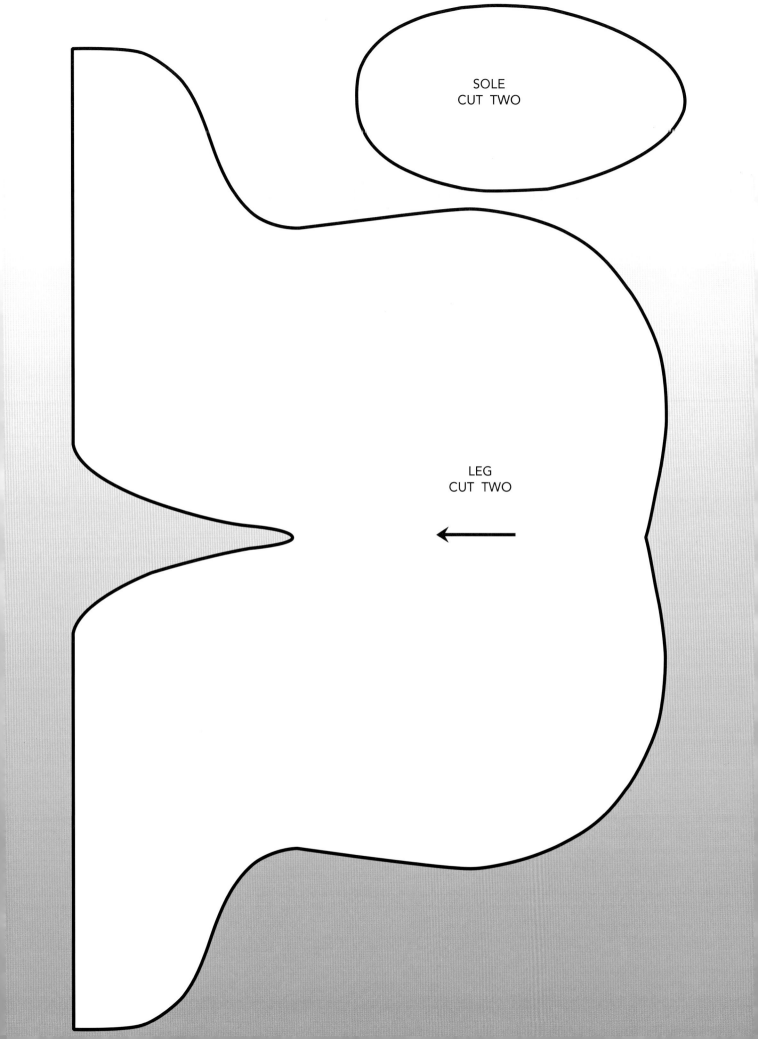

SOLE
CUT TWO

LEG
CUT TWO

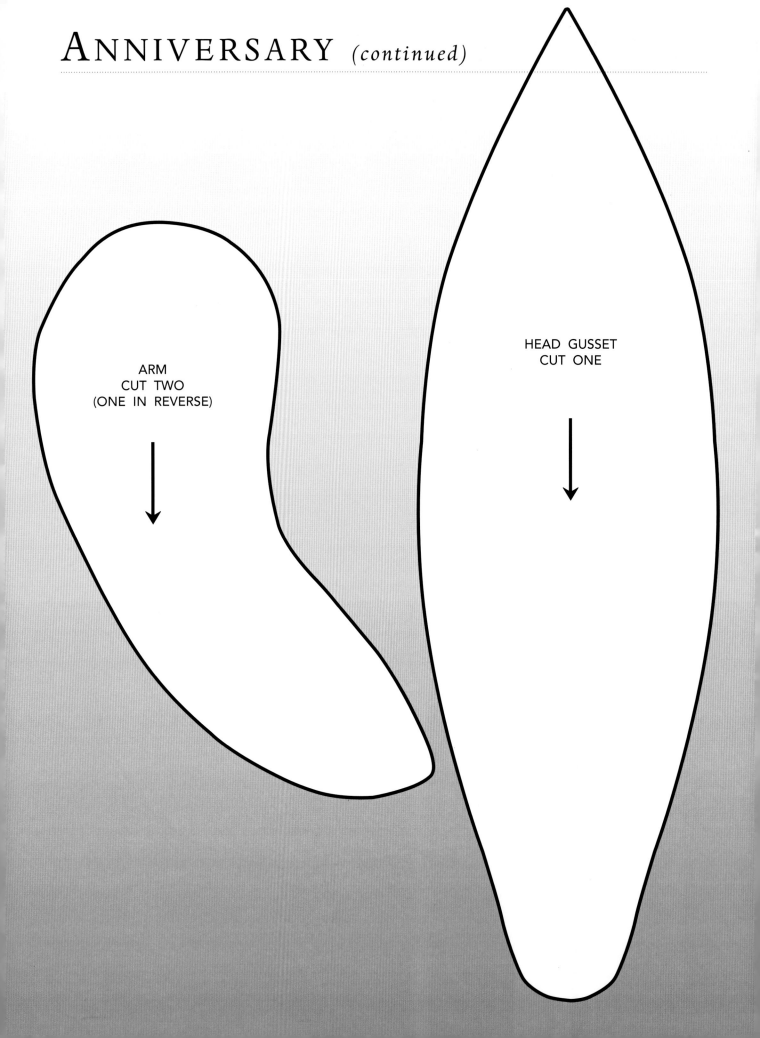

ARM
CUT TWO
(ONE IN REVERSE)

HEAD GUSSET
CUT ONE

Nathaniel

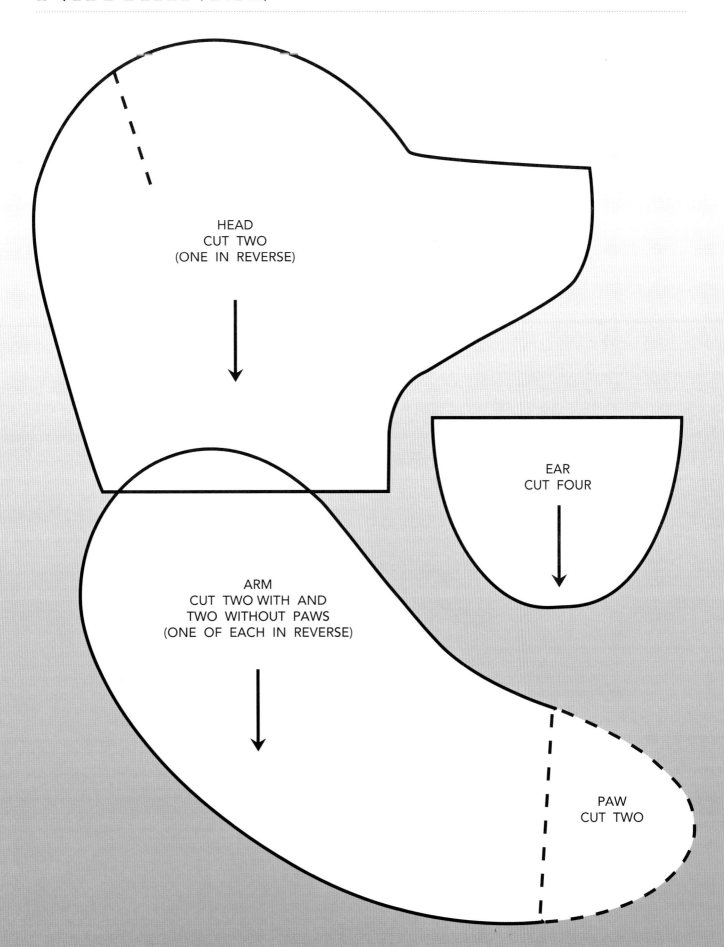

HEAD
CUT TWO
(ONE IN REVERSE)

EAR
CUT FOUR

ARM
CUT TWO WITH AND
TWO WITHOUT PAWS
(ONE OF EACH IN REVERSE)

PAW
CUT TWO

NATHANIEL *(continued)*

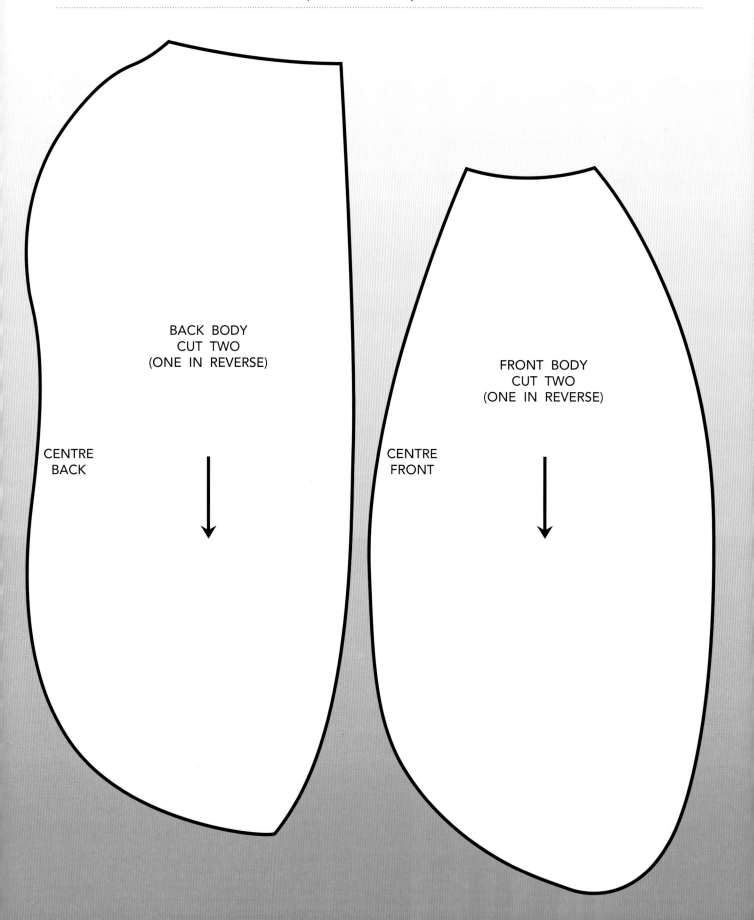

BACK BODY
CUT TWO
(ONE IN REVERSE)

CENTRE
BACK

FRONT BODY
CUT TWO
(ONE IN REVERSE)

CENTRE
FRONT

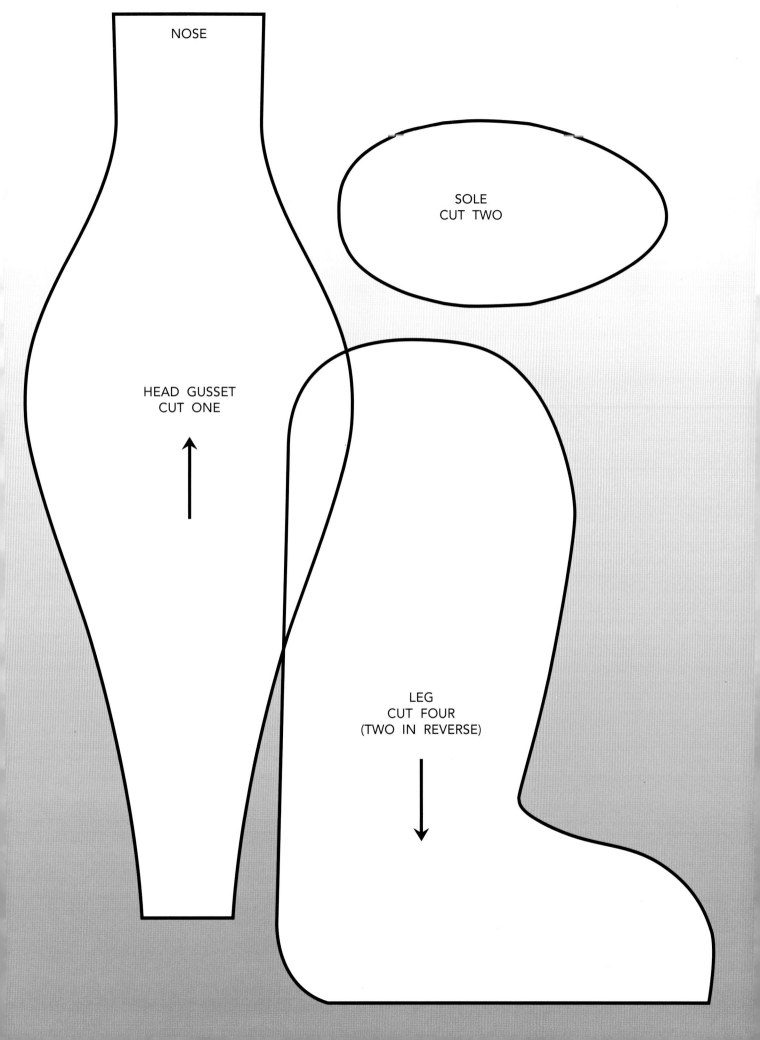

NOSE

SOLE
CUT TWO

HEAD GUSSET
CUT ONE

NOSE

LEG
CUT FOUR
(TWO IN REVERSE)

DAVID

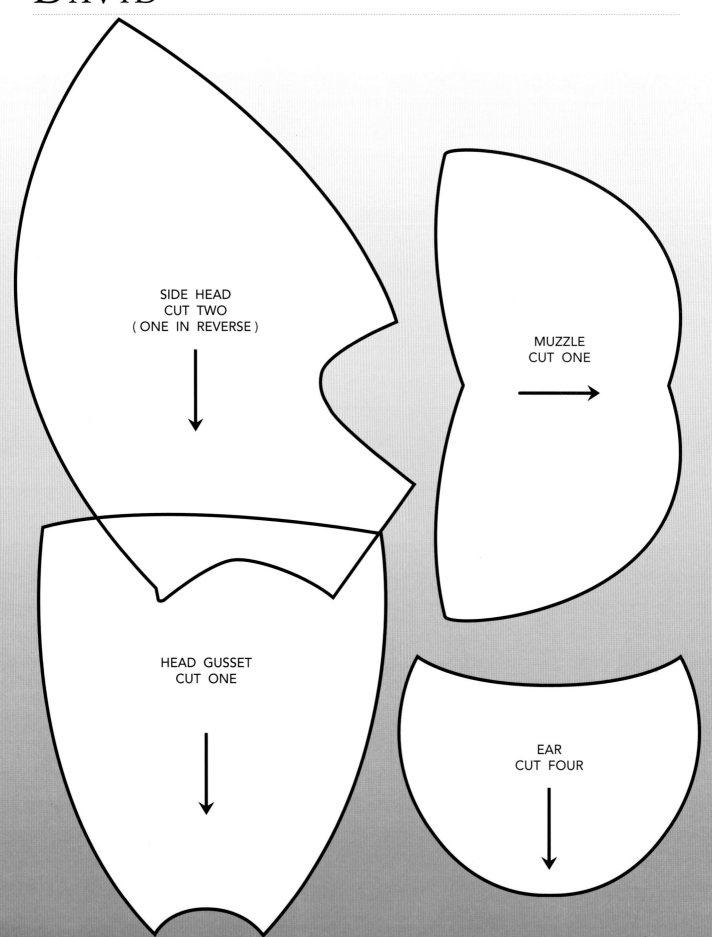

SIDE HEAD
CUT TWO
(ONE IN REVERSE)

MUZZLE
CUT ONE

HEAD GUSSET
CUT ONE

EAR
CUT FOUR

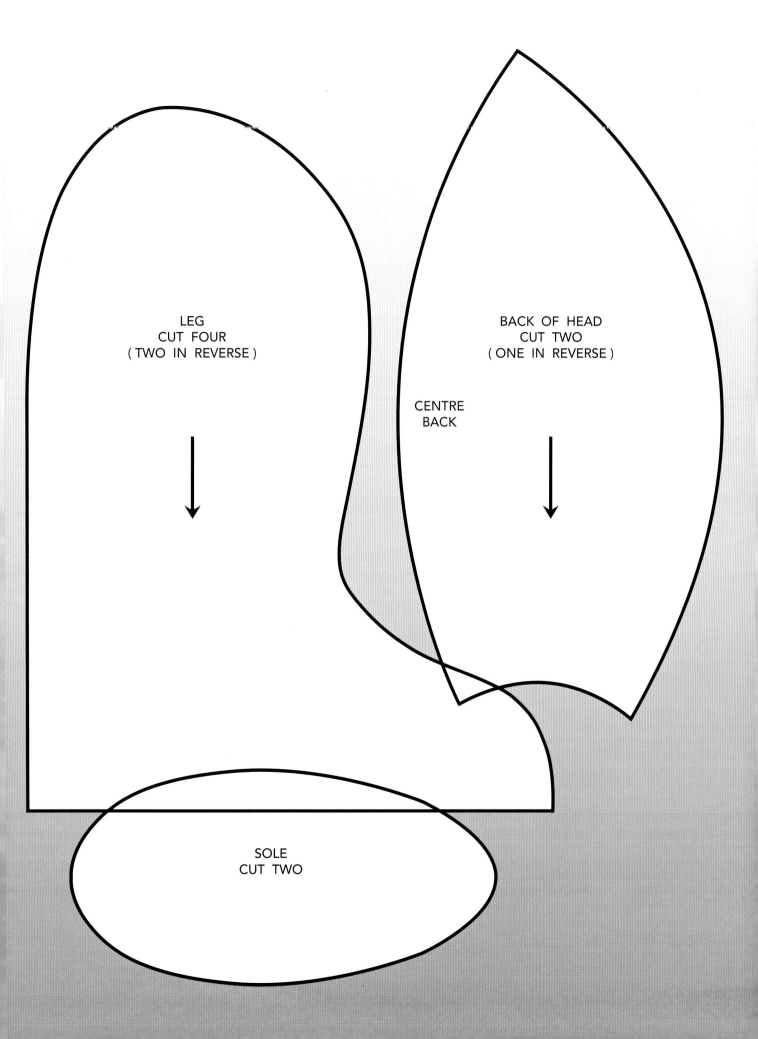

LEG
CUT FOUR
(TWO IN REVERSE)

BACK OF HEAD
CUT TWO
(ONE IN REVERSE)

CENTRE
BACK

SOLE
CUT TWO

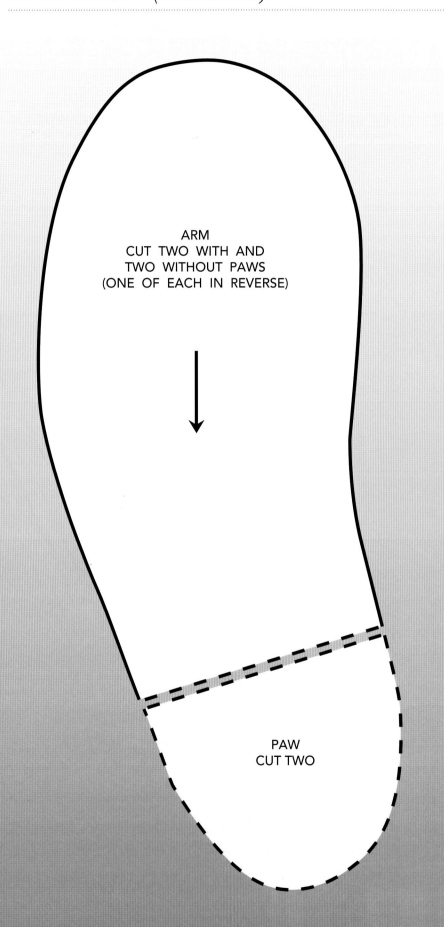

ARM
CUT TWO WITH AND
TWO WITHOUT PAWS
(ONE OF EACH IN REVERSE)

PAW
CUT TWO

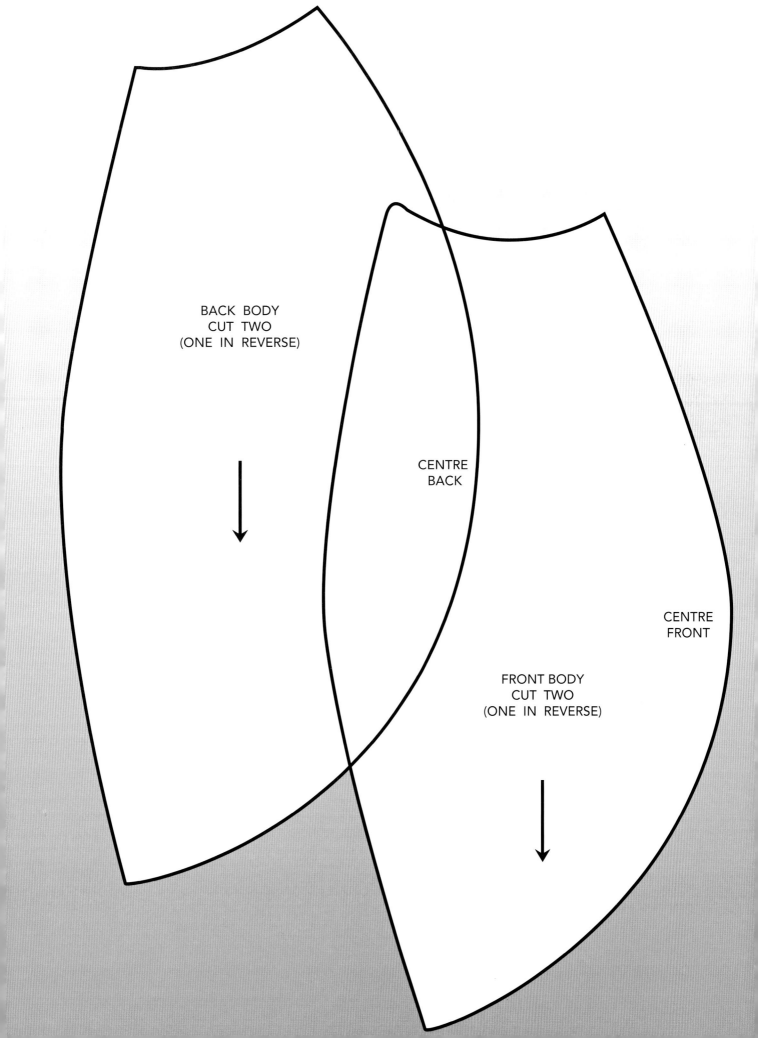

BACK BODY
CUT TWO
(ONE IN REVERSE)

CENTRE
BACK

CENTRE
FRONT

FRONT BODY
CUT TWO
(ONE IN REVERSE)

ROB ROY

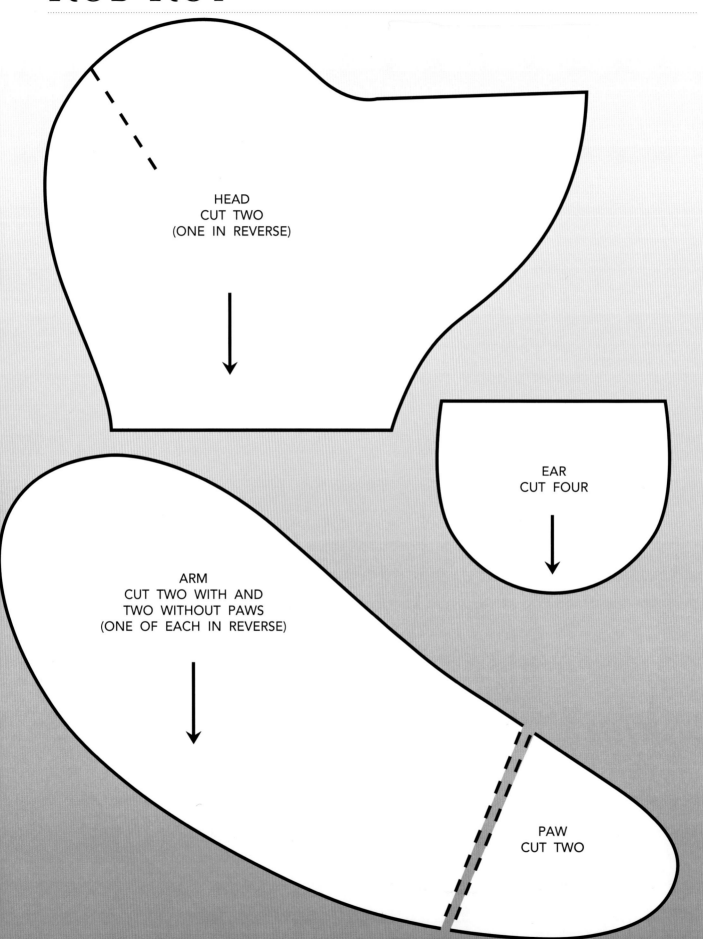

HEAD
CUT TWO
(ONE IN REVERSE)

EAR
CUT FOUR

ARM
CUT TWO WITH AND
TWO WITHOUT PAWS
(ONE OF EACH IN REVERSE)

PAW
CUT TWO

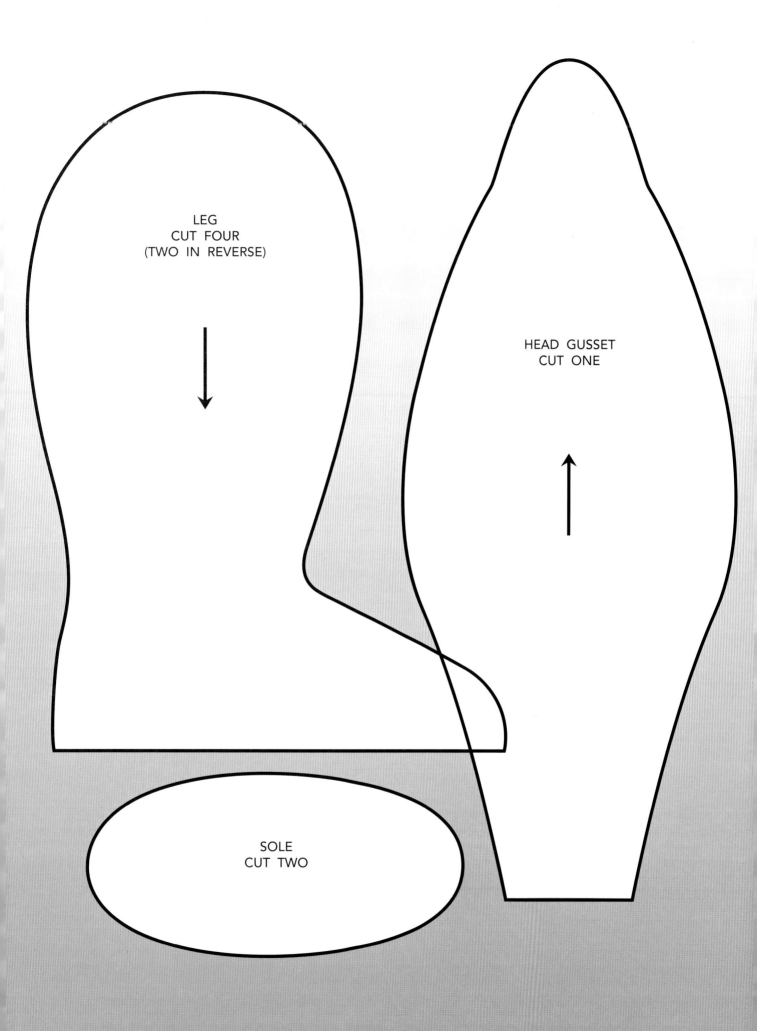

LEG
CUT FOUR
(TWO IN REVERSE)

HEAD GUSSET
CUT ONE

SOLE
CUT TWO

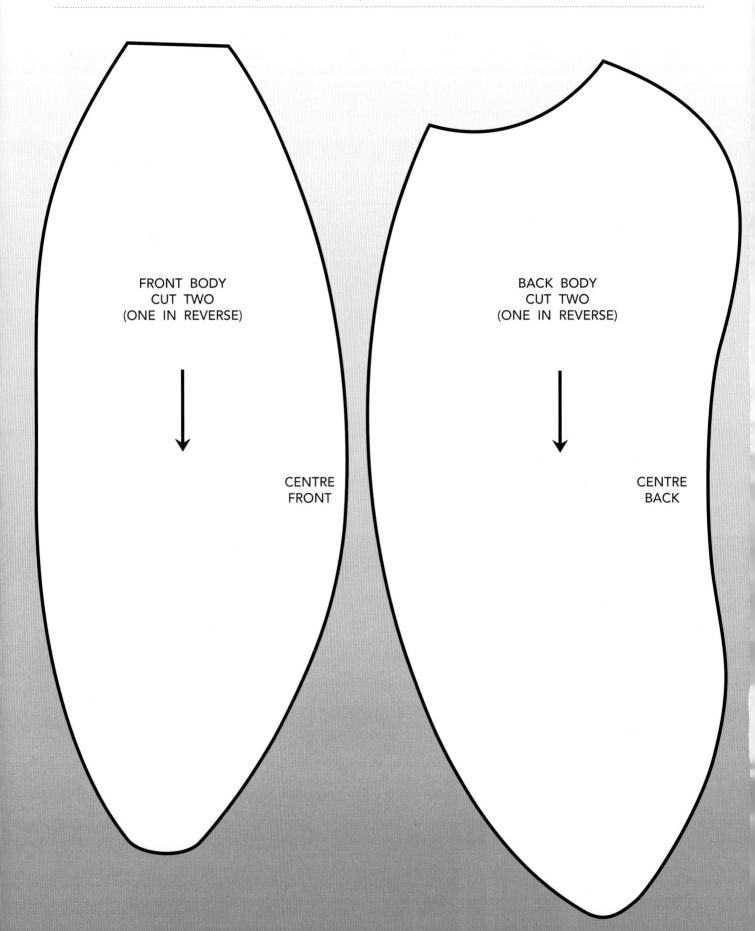

FRONT BODY
CUT TWO
(ONE IN REVERSE)

CENTRE
FRONT

BACK BODY
CUT TWO
(ONE IN REVERSE)

CENTRE
BACK